David Pye

The Nature and Aesthetics of Design

BARRIE & JENKINS
COMMUNICA - EUROPA

© David Pye 1978

First published
by Barrie and Jenkins Ltd. 1978
24 Highbury Crescent, London N5 1RX

ISBN 0 214 20375 1

Printed in Great Britain

Contents

1. Art and Science. Energy. Results   page 11
2. Invention and design distinguished   21
3. The six requirements for design   23
4. The geometry of a device   36
5. Techniques. Skill   43
6. Invention: analogous results   58
7. We can wish for impossibilities. Utility. Improvement. Economy   66
8. The requirements conflict. Compromise   70
9. Useless work. Workmanship   77
10. Architecture. Inventing the objects   82
11. 'Function' and fiction   85
12. The designer's responsibility   90
13. The aesthetics of design   96
14. Perception and looking   116
15. Taste and style   127
16. Originality   144
17. The common ground between visual art and music. What we really see   151

List of illustrations

Calligraphy ascribed to the Sung Dynasty   10
Die-sinking: Head of Arethusa 5th Century BC   11
Otto Lilienthal hang-gliding 1896   15
James Watt's 'Cabinet' steam engine. After 1800   20
The Tay Bridge Disaster   26
Japanese woodcut from Hokusai's *Hundred Views of Fuji*   28
The 'Cutty Sark'   29

The Erechtheum   31
Upper Yangtze trading Junk   40
Maudslay's bench lathe c.1810   49
Esso refinery, Fawley   71
Regulator clock by Benjamin Vulliamy 1780   72
'The weather in the space'. Church, Romney
    Marsh   82
'The weather in the space'. Chapel at
    Ronchamp   83
Former Monastery S. Maria d'Arrabida   92
Caol Isla distillery   97
Fisherman's basket   111
The face of the waters   112
Love and Chastity: Florentine School 15th
    century   115
Table, inlaid ivory, Italian early 16th century   119
Table, inlaid, Portuguese 17th century   119
Astrolabe by Anthony Sneewins 1650   128
Nocturnal, French late 17th century   129
Maudslay's bench lathe and cabinet   132
Colchester lathe   133
Contemporary chair by David Pye 1950   137
Chair by David Pye 1961   137
Art nouveau cabinet   138
Sideboard designed by Kaare Klint   139
Croft on Barra   140
Bows of fishing boat   140
Book display table   140
Longford cheese factory   141
Surrey farm waggon   141
First 1 in. micrometer calliper, Brown and
    Sharpe 1877   142
Micrometer calliper, Brown and Sharpe 1928   142
Japanese shears   144
Norris shoulder plane   145
French art nouveau cabinet c. 1900   146
Avignon by Corot   147
Chair designed by C. R. Mackintosh c.1897   148

Acknowledgements

I am particularly indebted to the late Mr Basil Taylor, Miss Patience Aspinall and Mr Colin Hayes for criticism and advice on the first edition: to Miss Joan Beach, who typed the manuscript of it: to those who gave photographs, which are individually acknowledged; and to Mr John Lewis, the editor, for help of many kinds and for the trouble he has taken over designing this book on design.

Preface

The original version of the first part of this book[1] sought to establish that design is always and necessarily an art as well as a problem-solving activity, but it went no farther. It did not discuss the art's aesthetics, nor the aesthetics of workmanship: and design can only become manifest through workmanship.

The second deficiency I attempted to make good in *The Nature and Art of Workmanship* (Cambridge University Press 1968) and the aesthetics of design are now discussed to the best of my ability in the second part of this book, the first part of it being a revised edition of *The Nature of Design*.

1. *The Nature of Design:* Studio Vista/Reinhold 1964.

Calligraphy: from *The Old Drunkard's Arbour.*
Ascribed to Sung Dynasty.
By permission of the Trustees, British Museum

1. Art and Science. Energy. Results

This book is about design and making, two of the principal human activities, and ones informed both by art and by science. If anyone thinks it important to civilisation that a common ground between art and science shall be found, then he had better look for it in front of his nose; for it is ten to one that he will see there something which has been designed.

The art of design, which chooses that the things we use shall look as they do, has a very much wider and more sustained impact than any other art. Everyone is exposed to it all day long. Indeed, in towns there is hardly anything in sight except what has been designed. The man-made world, our environment, is potentially a work of art, all of it, every bit of it.

As someone very properly said 'Art ain't all paint'. Die-sinking and calligraphy have each been rated of equal importance with painting in their day and place. Whether anyone now thinks design more or less important than painting is not a matter of importance. But it is important that design shall be good, if only because, unlike the fine arts, it is inescapable.

Although the importance of design is realised, the essential nature of the activity seems not to be understood except by designers, and they have not formulated what they know. It is not of the slightest use for us to ask 'what is good design?' until we can answer the question 'what *is* design?'

The thing which sharply distinguishes useful design from such arts as painting and sculpture is that the practitioner of design has limits set upon his freedom of choice. A painter can choose any imaginable shape. A designer cannot. If the designer is designing a bread knife it must have a cutting edge and a handle; if he is designing a car it must have wheels and a floor. These are the sort of limitations which arise, as anyone can tell, from the 'function' of the thing being designed.

Little is ever said which touches on the fundamental principles of useful design, and what is said is often nonsense. Most of the nonsense probably starts at the point where people begin talking about function as though it were something objective: something of which it could be said that it belonged to a thing.

The dictionary defines function as 'the activity proper to a thing, the mode of action by which it fulfils its purpose'. What (on earth) can that mean? Surely if there

Die-sinking: Head of Arethusa. Tetradrachm of Syracuse, 5th century BC
By permission of the Trustees, British Museum

11

were activities proper to things, and if things acted, and if they had purposes, Newton might have been relied on to take note of these facts? 'Function' will not square with physics. And if function is a fantasy, what of functionalism – the doctrine that form follows function?

What is the activity proper to a straight cylindrical bar of steel a quarter inch in diameter on cross section and four inches long? What function is this form following, or ought it to follow? What activity exclusively and distinctively belongs to this thing, is in other words proper to it? There it lies on the bench; what are we to say? – 'Well, it isn't active. You could make it active if you heated it enough. Otherwise it will not do anything unless the bench happens to collapse. Of course you could use it for an enormous number of different purposes, but then for nearly every one of them you could use something different equally well . . .' The question has still to be answered, 'what is the function of this thing?'

Now plenty of people do really believe that form can follow function; that if you thoroughly analyse the activity proper to the thing you are designing, then your analysis will provide all the information needed, and the design can be derived logically from the function. Plenty of people still believe that 'purely functional' designs are possible, and believe that they themselves produce them, what is more! But none of them has yet divulged what an analysis of a function looks like and what logical steps lead from it to the design. All you will get from them is talk about the purpose of the thing, which, as we shall see, is a statement of opinion and can never be anything else.

Someone will reply 'This is all pedantry. Think out what the thing has got to do, design it in the simplest form which will do that and there you have a purely functional design; and what is more it will look right.'

This sort of assertion raises three questions:

1 How do you determine what the thing you are going to design 'has got to do', what 'activity is proper to it', what 'it is for', what 'its purpose' is?
2 Having done so, does the information you have gained govern the design and determine its form, or does it merely guide it, restricting the choice of form and setting limits within which it can be varied at will?
3 What does 'purely functional' mean?

We shall have to consider the implications of all three questions at some length in the chapters which follow. We shall find that the answer to the first question is, 'arbitrarily'. The answer to the second question is 'it merely guides it', *for the form of designed things is decided by choice or else by chance; but it is never actually entailed by anything whatever*. Nothing in the realm of design ever 'looks like that because it has got to be like that' as some eminent person said on television. The answer to the third question is in practice, 'cheap', or else 'stream-lined', or else, more rarely, 'light'.

Anyone can verify by simple observation two important facts. The first is, that whenever humans design and make a useful thing they invariably expend a good deal of unnecessary and easily avoidable work on it which contributes nothing to its usefulness. Look, for instance, at the ceiling. It is flat. It would have been easier not to have made it flat. Its being flat does not make you any warmer or the room above you any quieter, nor yet does it make the house any cheaper; far from it. Since there is a snobbism in these things flattening a ceiling is called workmanship, or mere crafts-manship; while painting gods on it or putting knobs on it is called art or design. But all these activities: 'work-manship', 'design for appearance', 'decoration', 'orna-ment', 'applied art', 'embellishment', or what you will, are part of the same pattern of behaviour which all men at all times and places have followed: doing useless work on useful things. If we did not behave after this pattern our life would indeed be poor, nasty and brutish.

The second fact, which can be verified by simple observation, is that all useful devices have got to do useless things which no one wants them to do. Who wants a car to get hot? Or to wear out its tyres? Or to make a noise and a smell?

The concept of function in design, and even the doctrine of functionalism, might be worth a little atten-tion if things ever worked. It is, however, obvious that they do not. Indeed, I have sometimes wondered whether our unconscious motive for doing so much use-less work is to show that if we cannot make things work properly we can at least make them presentable. Nothing we design or make ever really works. We can always say what it ought to do, but that it never does. The aircraft falls out of the sky or rams the earth full tilt and kills the people. It has to be tended like a new born babe. It drinks like a fish. Its life is measured in hours. Our dinner table ought to be variable in size and height, removable altogether, impervious to scratches, self-cleaning, and having no legs. The motor car ought to stop dead, and no one in it be thrown forward, in the same instant that you press a button. We cannot console ourselves with the belief that such things are impossible. Who would ever have believed that a child could light a whole room by moving its finger?

Never do we achieve a satisfactory performance. Things simply are not 'fit for their purpose'. At one time a flake of flint was fit for the purpose of surgery, and stainless steel is not fit for the purpose yet. Every thing we design and make is an improvisation, a lash-up, something inept and provisional. We live like castaways. But even at that we can be debonair and make the best of it. If we cannot have our way in performance we will have it in appearance.

Few people, perhaps, will accept this. An old lady was seen to look skywards as one of the earliest flying machines passed overhead and was heard to say 'Of course, my dear, they'll never *fly*'. The blatantly obvious is seldom easy to believe! But one day the dictionary may read, 'FUNCTION. What someone has provisionally decided that a device may reasonably be expected to do at present'.

When any useful thing is designed the shape of it is in no way imposed on the designer, or determined by any influence outside him, or entailed. His freedom in choosing the shape is a limited freedom, it is true, but there are no limitations so close as to relieve him or the maker of responsibility for the appearance of what they have done. The ability of our devices to 'work' and get results depends much less exactly on their shape than we are apt to think. The limitations arise only in small part from the physical nature of the world, but in a very large measure from considerations of economy and of style. Both are matters purely of choice. All the works of man look as they do from his choice, and not from necessity.

The first part of this book was written in an attempt to answer the question: 'of what kinds, precisely, are the limitations on his choice and their causes?'

We are here concerned with devices; things designed

'The ability of our devices to get results depends less exactly on their shape than we are apt to think'. Otto Lilienthal hang gliding, 1896
Photo: Science Museum London

for use: buildings, ships, vehicles, tools, furniture, clothes, and so forth, and not with things designed solely for contemplation such as pictures and statues.

Of all devices designed for use it may be said that they are intended to get some result which was not there before; some objective and measurable result, such as a man warmer or cooler than before (building, clothes), a thing transported to a new place (ship, vehicle), a thing in two pieces which was in one (tool), a man supported who was self-supported (bed).

There is a distinction between the result of a device's being used and the purpose of it. The kind of result which, for example, cargo vessels are intended to realise is cargo transported overseas. All cargo vessels are, as a matter of ascertainable fact, designed, built, paid for and handled, to achieve *that kind of state of things*. As for the purpose of those vessels, if God knows all men's minds, then we may say that God alone knows what their purpose may be; for the purpose of a ship is any purpose imputed to it by any man. To the owner the purpose of the ship may be to make money. To the captain it may be to ply the seas. To the designer it may be to carry four thousand tons of cargo at ten knots. To the enemy it may be to compass his defeat. The purposes of things are the purposes of men and change according to who entertains them. They change, moreover, when a man's mind changes. My motor car has at present, perhaps, the purpose of taking the children to school. But I think, perhaps, that the time has about come when its purpose should change to housing the chickens. Then the purpose of my car is housing chickens and that is all about it. But the states of things, i.e. results, which that same car is capable of achieving are matters of fact, not of someone's whim, not affected by anyone's purpose. The fact that every device when used produces concrete, measurable, objective results, is the only sure basis for a theory of design. Any concept such as 'function' which includes the idea of purpose is bound to be an unsafe foundation; for purpose leaves commonplace factual affairs like results far behind.

Wherever there is a result there has been a change, and all changes in the world are produced by the passage of energy. Since an understanding of the nature of results is the key to an understanding of the nature of design, we shall have to take note of certain facts about energy.

The first fact is that energy is manifested in several different forms any of which can be transformed into another. Thus by means of a furnace the chemical energy of coal is transformed into heat energy. The heat energy, by means of a steam boiler, turbine, and generator is transformed into electrical energy. The electrical energy may be transformed by a lamp into the form of energy we call light, or by an electric motor it may be transformed into kinetic energy – the energy of movement – which is applied to move, say, a train; so that transport is an end result of the chain of transformations.

Any one of these forms of energy is capable of producing changes, changes in things; more exactly, redistributions of matter. The various ways in which matter can be redistributed are: shifting – that is to say, moving bodily; deforming – bending, stretching, compressing etc.; dividing – splitting, powdering, cutting, abrading, etc.; joining – welding, fusing, adhesion, etc.; change of state – melting, solidifying, vapourising. But all of them in the last analysis amount to shifting. Any redistribution of matter, any and every result other than a transformation of energy which a device can be used to get, amounts to a shifting of things or to a holding of them still, whether they be mountains, molecules or men.

Now whenever a change is made, by the passage of energy, and a result is left, this event takes place in a group of things. Things are always together. They do not exist separately and they cannot act separately. For present purposes we shall call a group of things in which a change takes place, a system. The word does not necessarily imply anything 'systematic' in the ordinary sense, or organised, such as a man, or a machine. It may do so, and often does, since any device is a system. But it need not. So far as the theory of energy is concerned, a heap of scrap iron is as good a system as an electronic computer, a house, or the state of Massachusetts.

Everything everywhere may be regarded as a component of a system. It is fruitless to consider the action of a thing without considering the system of which it is a component. This fact has a special importance for designers in various fields because they tend to think of things separately and to design them separately. We ought not to do this if we can help it. We ought at least to remind ourselves that we are concerned with a whole system even if we are only able to effect the design of one component. It is arguable that the locomotive engineers of the nineteenth century had more vision than the automobile engineers of the twentieth; for in the nineteenth century they conceived of the vehicle and its road as one system and designed them together.

It is well to remember that by the time-scale of the universe the shapes of all things and systems are as fugitive and evanescent as those of clouds driven before a gale, which coalesce and dissolve as they go. Energy is the gale. *Panta rhei*.

When energy in any of its several forms is put into a system of any kind, changes take place, both in the energy, which suffers transformations, and in the components of the system, where various redistributions of matter occur. The changes in such a system as a motor car and road, for example, are familiar enough: chemical energy turns into heat energy and that into kinetic energy; gases expand, parts of the car shift, parts vibrate, bearings wear, tyres wear, sound waves are generated, stones are thrown aside, and so on. Events of just the same kind occur in a heap of scrap iron if energy is put into that by, say, compressing it in a powerful press. Kinetic energy is transformed into heat energy; pieces shift, vibrate, change their shape, expand under heat, wear away or break up. In neither of these cases, nor in any other, is energy dissipated, in the sense of being lost. Energy is indestructible. When it passes through a system it is transformed but never lost. It ends up as heat, widespread and at a low temperature, and so is no longer accessible to our use, but it has not been destroyed.

When you put energy into a system you can never choose what kind of changes shall take place and what kind of results shall remain. God has already decided those things. All you can do, and that only within limits, is to regulate the amounts of the various changes. This you do by *design,* which is the business of ensuring that at least you get the change you want along with all the others which you don't, such as heat, noise, wear, and the rest. It is as though the world operated on the principle of 'truck'. If you want some of this then you must take some of that as well, even though you do not want it.

Whenever we design something we do so in order to get an intended result. Along with that we get unwanted results. The total of all the results together we may call the 'response' of the system to the in-put of energy. The particular things which are involved in the intended result itself, we may call the 'objects'. In the present discussion that word will be used to refer to a thing and not a thought.

Design – useful design, that is to say – is the business of adapting a known system so as to get at least the intended result, when energy is deliberately put in or admitted to the system. In structures, however, energy is constantly being put in by gravitation. Here the designer's purpose is not to get a particular result but to avoid getting one. He has to ensure that the response does *not* include at least one kind of change – shifting. He can, and must, put up with strain and deformation of various kinds, but shifting will not do at all.

We can never select the one result we want to the exclusion of all others, and neither can we select one source of energy to the exclusion of all others. There are all too many sources which supply energy we do not want. Design is concerned as much with averting the possible consequences of unwanted inputs of energy as it is with getting the intended results from energy which we can control. The sun persists in heating things; the wind blows things over; moth and rust corrupt; and, above all, gravitation never lets up. The architect is concerned almost entirely with uncontrollable sources of energy (except of course in the mechanical equipment of buildings); while all design of every kind is concerned in part with gravitational energy.

Let us now consider the system in the first diagram. Someone puts energy in by way of A, a hammer which hits B which hits C which is supported by the anvil D. Suppose that B is cold steel and C is red-hot steel. The intended result is presumably as in Fig. 2: from which we deduce that B is the tool and C the object. But now suppose that B is red-hot and C is cold. The intended result is now presumably as in Fig. 3, more or less. Previously we called B 'a tool' and C 'the object' or, probably, 'the job'. Now however we call C the tool and B the job. We judge by results. Devices of all kinds are classified by their results, not by their form. You cannot tell what result the system will produce until you have found out the relative hardness of B and C. The 'modes of action' of B and C or the 'activities proper to them', – their functions – are independent of their forms. I do not know how the functionalists managed to avoid noticing this fact, but they seem to have managed wonderfully well, considering.

These diagrams illustrate the fact that the designer can only ensure that the intended results do occur, by selecting certain properties for its components, namely those required by the nature of the result, of the objects, and of the energy put in. That in principle is his job.

From this it follows that shape is not really his primary concern at all. It also follows that, as everyone knows, it is possible to design things which cannot be made. I have designed an axe and a knife which are an immense improvement on anything of the kind which exists. Their edges are ground to a bevel of one degree and they keep their edge indefinitely. Unfortunately we cannot make them, yet. As for our present axes, they do not work. Axes are meant for cutting down trees, not for making a lot of piddling little chips.

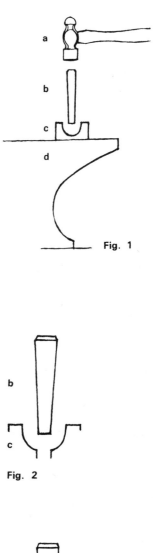

Fig. 1

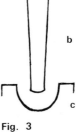

Fig. 2

Fig. 3

James Watt's 'cabinet' steam engine. After 1800
Lent to the Science Museum, London by A. Greg Esq

2. Invention and design distinguished

Although in many fields designers quite frequently make inventions, designing and inventing are different in kind. Invention is the process of discovering a principle. Design is the process of applying that principle. The inventor discovers a class of system – a generalisation – and the designer prescribes a particular embodiment of it to suit the particular result, objects, and source of energy he is concerned with.

The facts which inventors discover are facts about the nature of the world just as much as the fact that gold amalgamates with mercury. Every useful invention is a discovery about the way that things and energy can behave. The inventor does not make them behave as they do.

'A system of this kind' means, 'this way of arranging things'. There is a principle of arrangement underlying each class of device. In some cases, for instance Supports or Enclosures, it is extremely simple. In others it is not. An inventor's description of the essential principle of a more intricate device, might be worded as follows: 'If you have a wheel, and if at any place except the centre you fix to it a pin standing at right angles to the plane of the wheel, then (provided always that the system is properly designed) the wheel can be turned by the piston rod of a reciprocating engine. It must be linked to the piston rod by a connecting rod which is longer than the distance from the centre of the wheel to the crank pin. One end of the connecting rod must be hinged to the piston rod so that it is free to swing, and the other end must be pivoted on the pin so that the pin can rotate freely in it.'

The piston rod, connecting rod, and crank pin are 'the device'. The wheel is 'the object'.

For the sake of brevity this description of an invention for converting reciprocating motion into rotary motion has not been worded to cover all conceivable instances; and would no doubt have been worded better by a patent agent – whose job it is to write such things – but it will serve to illustrate the essential point that while the description is virtually complete and comprehensive, the accompanying diagram is very incomplete although easier to understand. The description describes the essential principle of the device, which is purely a matter of its arrangement. Almost every conceivable instance is covered by the description. The diagram on

Fig. 4

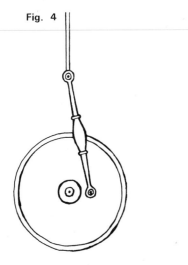

the other hand merely describes one particular embodiment of the invention. Someone failing to guess the essence of the invention from the diagram might suppose that the swelling in the connecting rod was essential, whereas the connecting rod can be of almost any shape provided it is properly designed. Shape is among the least important properties of a connecting rod, not much more important than colour. But for that matter shape is not all important even to a ball bearing. No two are the same shape and certainly none of them is spherical.

The description says nothing about the shapes of the components of the system. 'A wheel' it says. The wheel may be a Geneva wheel, of a complicated star shape. The pin could be triangular in section. The connecting rod could well be in the shape of a dragon. The hinge could be made of eel-skin like a flail's. And still the thing could work. The description says distinctly how the parts are related to each other in arrangement without saying what they are like. The relations between them which it describes are those which determine in what direction energy can and cannot be transmitted from one to another. Quite a complicated relation is often implied by one word. The word pivot, for instance, implies a pair of things one of which embraces the other but cannot, except by friction, transmit turning forces to it.

It is really rather remarkable that, while anyone can tell whether a thing is a pocket-knife because, presumably, anyone can recognise the principle of arrangement which constitutes the similarity between all pocket knives, no one can *visually* abstract that arrangement. We recognise it when we 'see' it embodied, we can describe it disembodied, but we cannot visualise it disembodied. (Recognition is further discussed in the chapter about 'Perception and Looking'.)

3. The six requirements for design

When a device embodying some known essential principle of arrangement such as we have discussed is to be adapted and embodied so as to achieve a particular result, there are six requirements to be satisfied:

1 It must correctly embody the essential principle of arrangement.

2 The components of the device must be geometrically related – in extent and position – to each other and to the objects, in whatever particular ways suit these particular objects and this particular result (Chapter 4).

3 The components must be strong enough to transmit and resist forces as the intended result requires.

4 Access must be provided (this is a special case of 2 above).

These four together will be referred to as *the requirement of use*.

5 The cost of the result must be acceptable.

This is *the requirement for ease and economy*.

6 The appearance of the device must be acceptable.

This the *the requirement of appearance*.

Design, in all its fields, is the profession of satisfying these requirements. The architect, however, has the additional task in effect of inventing the objects before he begins (Chapter 10).

The question we have to consider is: how far, if at all, does each of these requirements limit the designer's freedom of choice?

The first requirement, that the design must correctly embody the essential principle of arrangement, has already been touched upon in the first two chapters.

Various aspects of the arrangements of mechanisms are dealt with in the science of kinematics, which deals with motion or holding still without reference to force and mass; that is to say it concerns itself with the movements of the components of devices but not with their strength or substance. It is a first principle of kinematics that mechanisms which are kinematically identical may be dissimilar in appearance: which amounts to saying that although the mechanisms are of different shapes they may share the same essential principle of arrangement. The functionalists presumably did not hold with kinematics, or perhaps considered the function of a mechanism to be independent of its motion!

Neither in textbooks of kinematics nor in patent specifications are essential principles of arrangement

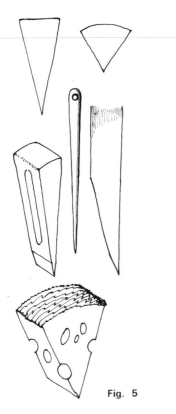

Fig. 5

stated in very general terms. The essential principle is ultimately concerned only with the capability of the things in the system to transmit forces of as yet unknown strength to the desired places and in the desired directions, and to modify them as desired. This capability depends on the arrangement of the things. But any statement of the essential principle is above all a general statement, and must therefore be concerned not with the arrangement of particular things but rather of things of certain classes. Although the classification is in fact based on the way the things transmit and modify forces, one would hardly think so when reading a statement such as that on page 21. The terms used appear to be particular and not general; and moreover they appear to define the shape of certain components rather closely. In such supposedly general statements as this we cheerfully talk about 'a pin', 'a rod', 'a hook', 'a cup', 'a wheel', 'a retort', 'a wedge'.

Let us suppose that such terms do in fact describe shape. Let us take the term wedge. What shape is a wedge? All the things in Fig. 5 are wedges. But which is *a* wedge? What indeed is a hook, a pin, a wheel?

Whatever else such terms refer to they do not refer to individual shapes. They are in fact terms referring to a class of arrangement of the matter within single things. A single solid thing, after all, is merely a slice of space with a few billion separate particles of this kind and that tottering about inside it. When we say a wedge we are indicating something about the way they are arranged. We are specifying a one-component system in fact. A fairly intricate device such as a safety-pin can be made of a single thing – a continuous wire – or, if desired, of several things.

The only way of closely defining the kind of arrangement of matter which we call a wedge or a hook would be by referring to the way it transmits forces. A hook will pull. A not-hook won't pull. Shape, individuality, doesn't come into it.

Shape, for us, is what gives individuality to things. All of us are extremely expert in recognising the individual character of shape in closely similar things such as human faces and hands of writing. The individuality of shapes is the stuff of art, whether in design, painting, or any other field. It is our present concern to find out how far the designer has freedom to give devices a chosen character of appearance, of shape. The essential principle which he must embody in the device he is designing sets limits merely to the extent that if the principle requires 'a hook' then not-hooks are excluded. But there is precisely an infinite range of possible shapes for a hook. The limitations on freedom of choice, so far, are nugatory.

The second requirement of those we enumerated, that the geometry shall be what the particular result entails, sets limits to the designer's choice of shape in ways which are best illustrated by a detailed example, and this will be found in the next chapter. It will be seen that the limits leave still an infinitely wide freedom of choice in the matter of shape.

It is worth noting that the essential principle of arrangement of every device was abstracted from, and is a generalisation based on, the first embodiment of the invention: an embodiment which, being real, had a particular geometry entailed by particular objects and a particular result. It is not always easy to make a true generalisation, separating the essential arrangement from the incidental geometry. This fact may have contributed to support the belief in 'functional' design. Because we visualise particular things, and can never visualise anything but what is particular, we fail to realise what an enormous latitude in choice of shapes we normally enjoy.

It would be most interesting to know the history of the idea that any device embodies an essential principle and so can be adapted to other results and objects than those in the first invention. There can be little doubt that this idea has sometimes been repugnant.

The third requirement is that the components must be strong enough to transmit the forces or resist them. The forces involved will originate both from the intentional input of energy as the system is used and also from unwanted sources of energy, in particular gravitation. This requirement obviously affects the size of each component, and in combination with the first two conditions, the essential principle and the geometry, it may begin to shove the designer in the direction of one shape rather than another. But in these days we are apt to forget what a very slight restriction on shape the calcula-

The Tay Bridge Disaster, 1879
Illustrated London News, Mansell Collection

tion of structures does actually impose. This is because we take it for granted first of all that the minimum amount of material ought to be used (a cheese-paring attitude which fortunately did not hold in, for instance, Rome, Athens, Venice, Chartres, and a few other places), and because we habitually use standard prefabricated components when making structures. The fact that you have calculated the minimum cross-section necessary to a member such as a column need not often prevent you from making it any shape you like.

Until very recent times, experience and rule of thumb based on it were the only things which could help a designer to decide what sizes the components of a system would need to be in order to give them adequate strength. In many trades, still, no other aids are used. But since exact methods of measuring changes have been evolved it has been possible to predict accurately what sizes will be adequate. The train of thought is of the form, 'We know that one unit of this stuff will support two tons. We want to support eight tons. How many units do we need? Four'.

In order to take the design of any structure even to the stage of a sketch the designer must first assume, roughly, the sizes which each part will need. Nowadays we shall verify these by calculation. In old days we should have been obliged to do so by trial. But we, like our ancestors, can only design if we are capable of making reasonable preliminary assumptions based on experience. There is no other way. The difference between their proceedings and ours is in the method of verification of the assumed sizes, not, at this stage, in the method of designing. Design always involves making trial assumptions based on experience. These may appear on paper or be carried in the designer's head. But the process is essentially a process of trial and error however the assumptions are verified, and this applies to many other assumptions besides those we make about strength.

It must be emphasised that design, of every kind, is a matter of trial *and error*. There are always some trial assumptions which no calculation or drawing can verify. Men can not foresee the future. Design, like war, is an uncertain trade, and we have to make the things we have designed before we can find out whether our assumptions are right or wrong. There is no other way to find out. When we modify our prototype, it is, quite flatly, because we guessed wrong. It is eminently true of design that if you are not prepared to make mistakes, you will never make anything at all. 'Research' is very often a euphemism for trying the wrong ways first, as we all must do.

Science has enabled us to make a few of the advances in technique which are obviously desirable, and these we shall presently discuss. It has not enabled us to predict the behaviour of people; which very many designers urgently need to be able to do. It has not enabled us to foretell what *will actually happen* in any particular case. It has enabled us to make better predictions about responses than our forefathers could make, but our predictions are still pretty shaky. We can not design a new spacecraft, or a railway train which does not rock, and get it right without trial and error. We design failures

'Some kind of immense washtub ...' Japanese
woodcut from Hokusai's
Hundred views of Fuji

大井川桶越の不二

chiefly because we cannot make reliable predictions about responses.

When a device is so designed that its component parts are only just strong enough to get the intended result without danger of failure, we may say it is in its minimum condition. This condition may be sought for other reasons than direct economy of material. In a large bridge, for example, the main problem may well be to make it carry its own weight. The traffic may be a mere flea on its back. Consequently every part of the bridge must be as small as possible consistent with its doing its work. The bridge must stand up, but only just. It is the small bridges which are massively built. The larger they are the lighter they usually seem, and are, relative to their size.

'Cutty Sark' in her dry dock at Greenwich.
Photo: The Times

It is a fair guess that arrows were the first things ever designed for a minimum of weight.

I suspect that the functionalists sometimes meant by functional design simply design aimed at the minimum condition for a device. In that case 'form should follow function' would mean that every system should be in its minimum condition, thus having certain limitations imposed on its form.

To say of most buildings that they shall be in their minimum condition is no more and no less arbitrary than saying that they shall be in the Corinthian order. Neither *diktat* has any bearing on how well or ill they do their job. If the system is in any adequate condition – and one adequate condition is the minimum condition – then it produces its intended result whether in the Corinthian order or not. It may be argued that the minimum condition is more economical. In houses it most certainly is not. The workmanship, research and calculation needed to design and achieve it will cost far more than the material saved.

In engineering on the other hand the minimum condition may really be worth having for the sake of economy in cost or in energy at work. But what applies to it does not apply to houses.

Among the shapes most often called 'functional' are those streamlined shapes which appear in parts of devices which penetrate things, for example a ship's hull under water, an aircraft, a spear head, some projectiles, an axe.

It is not easy to penetrate solids and fluids at any considerable speed. There are too many unwanted resistances in the response. When a minimum of resistance is required the geometry becomes very exacting and imposes very close limits to the designer's freedom of choice. There is not too much difficulty in getting any old shape of ship through the water at one knot, but some kind of immense wash-tub propelled at thirty knots will produce a very awkward response and take a vast amount of energy. If high speed or easy penetration is required then the unwanted parts of the response must be reduced to a minimum.

But in these designs, as in all others, compromises are invariably made. The visible shape of a streamlined craft depends as much on what you have chosen to streamline, i.e. to put inside it, as on the laws of nature.

Every make of aircraft differs in shape from every other.
  These 'functional' shapes designed for a minimum of change in the way of shifting air or water are as much chosen shapes as any other, and a minimum condition is as much a chosen condition as any other adequate condition. The reasons for the choice may be economic or aesthetic or defensive or silly or doubtless of many other kinds.

'The mark of economy in, literally, every stone'
the Erechtheum
Greek Government Tourist Bureau

The fourth requirement of use is that for access. We think of a device as a self-contained system, but of course no system is self-contained. Every device is a subsidiary part of a more extended system (which must contain among its other components, man). Since any device will have to become a component of a larger system or of several in turn, its geometry must be suited not only to its own proper result but also to the result of the extended system or systems. It follows that a prime requirement in the design of many devices is accessibility. The quay must allow the crane access to the ship's hold. The ship must draw no more water than covers the sill of the dock. The engines and their accessory devices must be disposed so as to allow access for the engineer's hands when he is maintaining them. The most familiar requirements for accessibility occur in buildings, and the art of planning them in its utilitarian aspect is largely concerned with affording the users of the building easy access to the several parts of it. Things do not invariably get in each other's way and access is sometimes so easily provided that the requirement is never noticed; but it can in other cases be most difficult to satisfy, for the most characteristic quality of modern devices is their complexity. Where there is complexity, requirements for access become difficult to satisfy, and impose distinct limitations on the designer's freedom of choice, (or, in some motor cars, evidently defeat him altogether).

The ultimate causes of complexity in devices nearly all lie in the requirement for ease and economy, but to trace the immediate causes and distinguish in principle the various very different ways in which they take effect would be a considerable undertaking. There is for example a clear distinction in principle between a mechanism and a mere aggregation of systems. A mechanism is a combination of distinct systems, but the result of each entails that of another. A thing like a stove is also a combination of distinct systems, but here although the result of one may or may not affect that of another, the result of none entails the result of another. One could remove the entire system for riddling the ashes and the entire system for regulating the draught, and still one could get the intended result somehow. There is no essential principle of arrangement for the systems *inter se* in an aggregation like a stove;

but in a mechanism there is. A mechanism is one system built up of systems. Most mechanisms however show an accretion of palliating systems also, such as anti-friction bearings and lubricating systems which could be omitted without affecting the essential arrangement of the system.

The fifth requirement, that for ease and economy, has very wide implications.

Theoretically it is possible to design for a result without the design being influenced in any degree, either directly or indirectly, by economy. In practice this does not happen. As will be seen, the most lavish and magnificent buildings show the mark of economy in, literally, every stone. The influence of economy in design is universal. But economy here implies something more than saving money.

Any change originated by man exacts a cost from him. The cost is reckoned in effort, trouble, time, often in running risk and enduring discomfort also. Adam found this out. 'Economy' as used in the present essay must be understood as referring primarily to this unpleasant catalogue and only secondarily to the money which we pay to avoid enduring it; for when we pay a price in money for a device, as a rule we are paying directly or indirectly to escape the natural cost in effort or discomfort, trouble, time or risk, of the result which the device gives.

The great majority of devices simply enable us to get cut-price results. There are really rather few devices which make it possible to get results which without them would be unattainable. The only such devices in the realm of transport, for instance, are the vessel, the raft, the aircraft, hovercraft and rocket. No form of land transport qualifies; all are merely palliative. One can walk.

Economy is the mother of most inventions, not necessity, unless in the sense of poverty and hardship. A requirement for convenience is simply a diluted requirement for ease and economy.

The consequences of the search for 'improvement' in devices are manifold. Perhaps the most obvious consequence is seen in the engineer's preoccupation with producing machines of higher efficiency, with less waste of power in friction; and in the importance in most manually driven machines of a high mechanical advantage; for we would all rather use a long lever than a short one. Such good engineering in the service of economy does impose limitations on the designer's freedom of choice of shape, but only very loose ones, for they mostly affect size alone. The lever is a fair example. The fact that you must make it long prevents you only from designing something short and thick while it leaves you an infinitely wide choice in other directions.

The more remote consequences of the search for cheaper results exert much more effective limitations than these; but the limitations which result from cheapening the manufacture of devices are far and away the most stringent of any. A low retail price in the shop often overrides every other consideration in design.

The requirements of use are imperative. If they are not complied with the device does not give the result. The requirements of economy are on a different footing, for the amount of weight given to them is a matter of choice.

All possible useful results except transformations of energy are shifts – shifts of particular things, large or minute, over particular distances in particular directions. The things, the distances, and the directions are legislated for by the requirements of use. But the speed of the shift, the energy needed to produce it, the amount of energy wasted in the process, the unwanted changes which accompany the shift, the labour or distress exacted from people, all these are legislated for by the requirement for ease and economy.

It seems to be invariably true that those characteristics which lead people to call a design functional are derived from the requirements of economy and not of use. I have found no exception. Streamlining, omission of ornament, exposure of structural members, 'stark simplicity', all of these derive directly or indirectly from requirements of economy (which is not to say that they do in fact give economy!). A result, though not always at an acceptable cost, can always be got without these characteristics. They are inessential. In some cases indeed they are as much features of style as any overt system of ornament.

A thing may be called 'purely utilitarian' if it is designed so as to comply with the requirements of use, and of ease and economy, but ignoring the requirement of appearance. No such thing really exists; for nothing can be made without some concession, however slight and unwitting, to the requirement of appearance any more than a human being can be entirely amoral.

Work done solely for the satisfying of the requirement of appearance may be called 'useless work'. Useless, of course, does not mean worthless.

The sixth condition is that the appearance of the device must be acceptable. This conflicts headlong with the requirements of economy and it is heartening to see how so many designers and manufacturers consistently expend useless work on satisfying it. Smoothness and all the qualities of surface finish, flatness, straightness, fairness of curves, neat fitting, neat detailing at junctions, all the qualities of appearance which decent workmanship produces, are to be seen still in immense numbers of the things of all sorts which men make; and almost all of these graces could be omitted or made worse without any loss of effectiveness in the devices which exhibit them. They are taken so much for granted that one would think people supposed that they were achieved automatically. No credit for them is given where credit is due. There is no realisation that they are an affair of art, and not less important than design in the large, for without them the best of design is entirely wasted so far as appearance goes. A surprisingly large proportion of manufacturing time in nearly every field is in fact taken up with useless work catering for the requirements of appearance.

The requirement of appearance imposes very distinct limitations on the designer's freedom of choice of shape in the large. This is done through the medium of styles of design, which confine him to a fairly narrow canon of shapes. It can be argued that design has invariably exhibited styles because some clear limitations on freedom of choice are psychologically necessary to nearly all designers. When design gets too easy it becomes difficult. Styles provide these desired limitations when, as so often, the requirements of use and economy do not impose limitations which are close enough. This point is enlarged upon in the chapter about 'taste and style' and the whole question of the requirement of appearance is discussed in chapters 12 to 16.

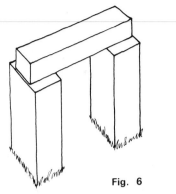

Fig. 6

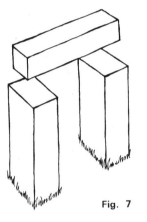

Fig. 7

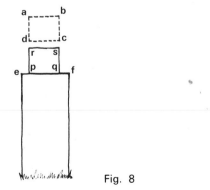

Fig. 8

This chapter explains in detail how the second of the requirements of use, that the geometry of the system shall suit the particular result intended, affects the appearance of the design. It also continues the discussion of invention.

Suppose that by the use of a lever we intend to raise a beam already standing on two piers. We want Fig. 6 to become Fig. 7, using blocks to hold the beam up another foot and a half (or cubit, by the look of the picture!) We propose to do this with a lever, by adding that to the existing system. Fig. 8 shows the existing system end-on, and the intended new position of the beam in dotted lines. Now if we simply get a lever, shove one end under the middle of the beam, take care that the fulcrum is below the lever, and sit heavily on the other end, it will be a remarkable bit of luck if the beam shifts from PQRS to ABCD. It will probably shift, if it shifts at all, from PQRS to almost anywhere else. Embodying the essential principle of arrangement is, by itself, no guarantee of getting any particular intended result. In fact we shall find, by trial and error, that no lever can ever shift the beam to position ABCD. It is impossible. But we may be inspired to realise that a lever system can be used to shift the edge of the beam, its arris, to position C and that if we do this and slip in the blocks below the beam when we have done so, it will fall to position ABCD, turning as it does so, when we take away the lever (Fig. 9).

We therefore decide to achieve the end result by way of an intermediate result. Now for this particular intermediate result, which is the beam shifted from position PQRS to position JGHC, Fig. 9, we shall have discovered that the geometry is fairly exacting. The fulcrum, for example, must be in a line which bisects the line CQ at right angles. If it is above this line the arris Q will be shifted to the left as it rises up; if below this line it will be shifted to the right; and in neither case can it reach the point C.

Now a lever cannot be a line. It has thickness. But in the new configuration of the system the base of the beam will by lying on the top of the lever, and the fulcrum must lie in the same plane as that. Hence the lever must be cranked or shaped like a dog's hind leg (Fig. 10). The geometry has begun to impose limitations on the shape of the system. But the limitations are by

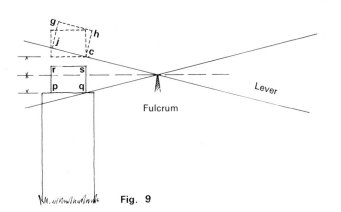

Fig. 9

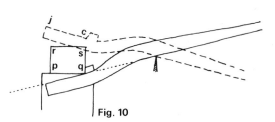

Fig. 10

no means severe, for the shape of the lever between the beam and the fulcrum can be almost anything, so long as it allows the fulcrum to lie in the line JC produced. It cannot be straight, but it can be of an infinite variety of shapes, and have dragons and small coils of rope carved on it if so desired.

The process of design which has produced it is trial and error – conducted in imagination and with the aid of drawings. There is no other way of arriving at it. However skilled the designer may be, he can only discover what geometry is needed by making assumptions, that is to say, imaginary trial arrangements. In this case however he can verify most of his assumptions by using theory, namely his knowledge of geometry, instead of actually building a trial prototype of the device.

I had intended to end the discussion of this example here. But having written the preceding paragraphs with the system in my mind's eye and illustrated only by a scribble in the margin, I thought it would be as well to make a more complete sketch of it as a memorandum for Figs. 6–9 which I should have to draw sooner or later. I accordingly did so, and was annoyed but not much surprised to find that I had overlooked something. The system as I had described it would not, in all probability, give the intended result; for when the lever starts to lift it touches the arris of the beam Q which from that time onwards must remain in the same place on the lever which it first touched, otherwise it will never arrive at C. But that point on the lever will swing through an arc of a circle convex towards the left of the picture as the beam is lifted (Fig. 11); while if the beam pivots, as it must, on the arris P during the early part of the lift

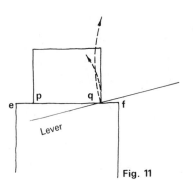

Fig. 11

(at which time only the other arris Q is in contact with the lever) the beam rotating about P will swing through an arc which is convex to the right. Consequently either P must slip to the left on top of the pier or Q must slip to the right along the lever. We cannot allow the latter, because if Q slips at the start it cannot reach its intended position at the finish. Therefore we must ensure that P slips to the left, or else ensure that the beam is lifted off without rotating, by cranking the lever still more (Fig. 13).

I thought, when I saw this, that for purposes of illustration, it would be better to abandon this example, which was a rather far-fetched concoction at best, and was getting complicated by too many snags, so that it would not bring out the important points as I had intended. But designing is delightful, while thinking of apposite examples and carefully describing them is hard work. So it came about that rather than get down to the hard work, I started without any conscious intention of doing so, to redesign the system so as to eliminate the snags; and it was soon done. When I had done it I thought that this after all was a good example to use, because I could describe the fairly typical train of thought which I had just gone through and thereby show something more about the nature of design.

The train of thought went somewhat as follows: 'Here is the difficulty of the intersecting arcs, and it is not going to be the only one. As the picture stands (Fig. 10) the beam is real and pretty heavy, the fulcrum is a mere notion of a knife edge floating in the air, and the lever is something between a diagram and a bit of wood, a bad bit of wood at that. If it happens to have been grown to that shape it will do the job, but it will take a long time to find a grown crook like that and the time will cost too much. But if it is made by cutting it out of a plank – supposing we can get a sound one large enough – it will be short grained and weak at the crook. What is more the fulcrum looks horrible. The lever will ride about and slip when we up-end it. The whole thing looks horrible, and why on earth don't we use a hoist? Because we are writing a book. Then what can be done with the lever? A block fixed at Q will prevent the beam slipping to the right. So P will slip to the left. So there will be a horizontal thrust on the pier trying to push it over and likewise on the fulcrum trying to push that

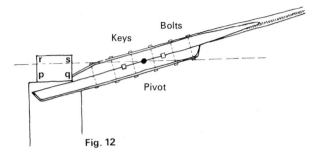

Bolts

Keys

r s

p q

Pivot

Fig. 12

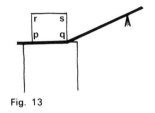

r s

p q

Fig. 13

over in the opposite direction. But the fulcrum will be on some sort of trestle, and we could shore up the pier if necessary (and it will not be necessary) so we can take care of the thrust. But the beam will not slip on the piers any too easily. We are picking it up at the middle of its length. If it slips on one pier and not on the other it will slew round. And what if both ends stick? But we can lift it slowly and have men with crowbars to edge it along so that both ends do slip, and slip together.

Then the lever will look like Fig. 10 and will not be any the better for it, in our opinion.

At this point we have the familiar brain-storm which is the special fascination of designing. We see – not think out, but see, all complete – a way of eliminating all the difficulties in one move and making a workman-like looking job into the bargain. What we see is Fig. 12. The lever is made up of two squared timbers held together by bolts (we afterwards substitute iron straps round the timbers). There are crossgrained hardwood keys in case the timbers try to slide along each other. There is a hole bored through which will take the fulcrum. The fulcrum is to be a cylindrical steel bar making an easy fit in the hole, in fact a pivot. Thus the necessary arrangement is provided for; the fulcrum is in the right place. The block is provided by the end of the upper timber, and the lever has its strength where it needs it most – near the fulcrum. All this we seem to see, suddenly, without conscious thought as a preliminary. We have killed all the birds with one stone.

The thinking has not been conscious, but it must have been done; for this design, like the analysis of the difficulties which preceded it, is evidence that we have a considerable knowledge of the kinds of response which occur in lever systems. We know the lever will bend.

Upper Yangtze Junk. A yuloh can be seen on deck
Crown copyright, Science Museum, London

We know it will tend to bend most at the fulcrum. We know too that if the fulcrum is to be a pivot penetrating the lever, then the best place to make the hole is midway between top and bottom. In that place the lever will be very little weakened.

We know all this, and know that we know it. The design has evidently been somewhat informed by this knowledge. But this is not the only design which would work. It is safe to say that no two designers using timber would design the lever in quite the same way. Making a doubling round the fulcrum was certainly not in our head when we set about designing the lever. I cannot swear to that. I cannot be sure that I have never seen such an arrangement. But I am certain that I did not have that idea consciously available in the same way that my rather imperfect recollection of the theory of beams was consciously available.

Where then did the idea of the doubling round the pivot come from? There is a certain element of invention or creation in the idea. Joining timbers by lapping or doubling is commonplace. Pivoting timbers on a bar through the middle is commonplace. But the idea of making a joint in a lever precisely at the point where it needs most strength is by no means commonplace. Moreover the act of neatly killing several birds with one stone, as we have done here, is not commonplace. It is in its degree ingenious.

But I do not believe that this or any such ingenuity is unprompted. Invention involves an antecedent of some kind.

In the present instance, when I set out to trace in my unconscious mind the antecedent for the doubled lever I found that there was persistently in my mind's eye a picture of something not only doubled but also crooked (Fig. 14). I realised that this was probably a recollection of an oar, called a Yuloh, used in China for sculling Junks and Sampans by the stern. The analogy then became apparent. The Yuloh, being an oar, works like a lever. It has a doubling in it which serves to make it crooked, *and it is pivoted at or near the doubling*. It is pivoted in a different way from our lever and produces a different though analogous result. The 'creative' act was the unconscious selection of the Yuloh out of all the innumerable devices stored in a designer's memory, as an analogous device to this very different

Fig. 14

Pivot

lever. Fig. 14 shows a Yuloh.

It is of course possible that I have unconsciously produced the Yuloh as a cover for unconsciously lifting someone else's invention of a doubled lever (which would be pretty ingenious in itself!). It is also possible that this way of working is a personal eccentricity of mine. But I do not believe in either possibility. I believe that this is the normal process of inventive 'creation'.

5. Techniques. Skill

We have briefly considered how far the shape of things we use is influenced by the requirements of use and economy and access. We must now consider the influence of technique. In doing so we shall find that the influence on shape of technique, *per se*, is small. Nearly all the so-called technical limitations on design are limitations not so much of technique as of material or, once more, of economy. We must distinguish between 'limitations' set by our unwillingness to incur work and trouble on the one hand, and real limitations set by our inability as workmen on the other. A competent workman nowadays may fairly say to a designer, 'Design what you like in the material I use, and I can make it, no matter what its shape may be'.

We are so reluctant to acknowledge that economy has been a major influence on the design of even the most splendid things which men have made, that we often say 'better' when we mean 'cheaper'. 'Work Study' is double-speak for Cheapness Study. Its basic principle that there is one best way of doing any operation in a factory, is untrue. It may well be true that there is one cheapest way.

Our insistence on doing useless work is continually in headlong conflict with our insistence on economical technique, which is simply the elimination of useless work. It is a most diverting spectacle to see the experts in work study exercising their considerable ingenuity to find the one cheapest way of doing operations which could perfectly well be dispensed with; for example, getting shiny surfaces on furniture. The 'one best way' of doing things like that is not to do them.

A technique embraces a group of systems which cause some specified change in the characteristics of pieces of material – any material.

Any material has certain characteristics – hardness, strength, ductility, stiffness etc. – and a certain amount of each is peculiar to any given kind of material. But material as such does not exist. Only things, *pieces* of material, exist. Man's earliest essays in using things were doubtless made by using the pieces of material as he found them. He had no techniques with which to alter either the characteristics of the material such as hardness or strength, or the characteristics of the piece, such as shape and size.

We no longer have to take the characteristics of the

piece as we find them. We have by now several effective techniques for altering these: wasting, forming, casting, and constructing. But we still have to take the characteristics of the material much as we find them, for we have not yet any thoroughly effective techniques for altering these, for processing materials.

Processing material means altering its properties, as in smelting or in hardening steel by heat, or making wood-wool out of wood, or fibre out of glass, or powder out of a solid, or cement out of mud. Wasting techniques are those which involve carving away a piece of material until the shape you want remains. Sawing, milling, planing, turning, punching, are examples. Construction means making a whole out of parts, by connecting them. Connection may be by interpenetrating, as in a carpenter's joints or a rivetted joint, or by interlocking, as in spinning or weaving, or by welding, or by jointing with an adhesive. Forming means changing the shape of a piece by bending, pressing, forging etc. Casting means pouring a liquid into or over a mould, which liquid subsequently hardens having taken the shape of the mould. Polishing is hardly a separate technique according to the usage here since it is a combination on a minute scale of wasting and forming (or, put another way, the function of a polishing tool is abrasion and melting!).

As things stand today the second and third of these techniques are very highly developed. It is almost true to say that one can cut any shape out of any material, and join anything to anything. The fourth and fifth techniques are also highly developed where they are applicable. But their application is limited because the first technique, processing, is still rudimentary.

The only considerable technical limitations on design are imposed by our ineptitude at processing material. We are still obliged to take most materials as we find them with all their natural properties and to improvise things out of what we find. In primitive woodworking one looked for a branch or root already grown to about the shape one wanted. With our primitive processing techniques we are obliged to do likewise in selecting materials. The technological advances of the next age will be in processing. We already see forerunners in our synthetic and reinforced composite materials.

Meanwhile for lack of adequate processing techniques

we are limited to materials which have fixed, arbitrary, combinations of properties. One can have a material which is hard, tough and stiff but only if it is also heavy, cold, opaque, and liable to rust – steel. One can have a material which is immune to rust, and is light and warm, and which is fairly hard, tough, and stiff, but only if it is unstable – wood. We can nearly always find some material with the one property we want, but we have no control over the concomitant properties of it; in other words over the total response. The truck agreement which compels us to take properties we do not want along with those we do applies particularly in technique. We can vary the tensile strength, say, of a component exactly as we wish, by first selecting a material which has fair tensile strength and then proportioning the cross section of the component to the tension force in it. What we cannot do, is to vary the other properties associated with the material we have chosen. The thicker we make the component the heavier it gets, but we should like it to get lighter as it gets thicker. What we need are more processing techniques which would enable us to vary properties of components independently of each other, and more techniques to vary them locally without altering size and shape, as has been done with steel for centuries, by hardening and tempering it.

Deficiency of technique is here a real limitation on the shape of things, even though in practice not a very severe one. It seems unlikely that this deficiency will ever be entirely made good.

There is also a serious deficiency in techniques for preventing corrosion and other such unwanted changes: again a deficiency in processing. Why should metals need coating?

The choice we make among our present range of materials may be directed not only by knowledge of the responses associated with them, but also in many devices, by the sizes in which the materials are obtainable.

Between the remaining four kinds of technique there is very little we cannot do. We cannot drill a serpentine or spiral hole but we can make one by casting or constructing. Cutters, abrasives and flames of various kinds will get through anything we know of, and we can control them. These techniques are inept only in respect of size. We cannot handle mountains or molecules very easily, though in optical work we can cut to a few millionths of an inch and we are getting better at handling small sizes, as micro-circuits show. But we can still do nothing very effective with any piece of material unless it has at least one relatively large dimension. Nor can we do anything effective with very large pieces. The technique of construction has been built up partly to make up for deficiencies in wasting, casting and forming techniques, but obviously very much more to circumvent our difficulties in handling large objects.

We may say then, as a fair generalisation, that wasting, constructing, forming and casting techniques taken together are so versatile that they impose, *per se*, hardly any limitations on the shape of what can be designed, but that they do impose limitations on the size of it.

The influence on shape which is exercised, not by technique, but by cheapness of technique, is enormous, and particularly so in the field of construction, which we shall consider first.

A flat surface will touch any other flat surface at all points. No other shape of surface will touch every other surface of similar shape at all points. A hemisphere, for instance, will only touch a hemispherical hollow at all points if it has the same radius as the hollow hemisphere; i.e. if the surface is of the same size. The flat surfaces need not be of the same size. Thus a mason building a wall need not fit each stone he lays to the stone below it. Having cut all his stones to flat surfaces first, he knows that any stone will bed steadily on any other without having to be fitted to it individually.

The versatility of flat surfaces is not commonly seen in nature. Stones which cleave under frost exhibit it; but the breadth of its application was a discovery of man's, and one of his most valuable, for it enabled him to reduce the cost of construction in all materials very considerably. An extension of the discovery was that if the components of a structure were 'squared', i.e. were given two flat surfaces at right angles, then they would not only touch each other at all points of the adjacent surfaces, but would also both do the same to a third component.

We take all this very much for granted. Any house and its contents, and the toy bricks on the nursery floor, showed us this before we could talk. The extraordinary rigmarole which I have had to use in writing about it is perhaps evidence that we take it as part of the natural order of things, which it is not. We have no colloquial word specifically for 'making a surface fit another by touching it at all points'. We very rarely need such a word. If we want things to fit in that particular way we give them flat surfaces and they do it automatically without our taking any further trouble. The boat builder cannot do this. He has a word. He speaks of making his curved surfaces 'fay' with each other. In some trades curved surfaces are said to 'mate' with each other.

Now the human hand does not take kindly to making things straight and still less kindly to making them flat and square, in any wasting technique. However, by testing from time to time with a straight edge, try-square and winding sticks, it can be done. But the labour of doing it, freehand, is really not very much less than the labour of making the first component any shape but flat and then fitting the second to it. The one serious disadvantage in that procedure as compared with freehand flattening is that the second component must be 'offered up' to the first from time to time in order to see whether it is getting near the right shape. In masonry this offering up was excessively laborious, and so the mason preferred to square his stones, and he did it virtually freehand. The brickmaker did likewise, but for him it was easy, once he had made a flat surface on which to form all his bricks. The carpenter also squared his timbers, but he did not work freehand. He applied the principle of the jig, and gradually extended it.

The most familiar example of a jig is a ruler. A jig is an appliance for guiding a tool in a predetermined path, independently to a greater or less extent of the operator's skill. A joiner's plane is essentially a chisel fixed in a flat jig, so that it flattens a surface with the use of much less skill and trouble than the chisel alone would require. But even the separate chisel, having its face flat, partly jigs itself once the cut has been started; and so did the carpenter's side-axe and saw.

Rotary motion of the tool or work piece acts as a jig. Any old bit of iron will bore a perfectly circular hole, and a remarkably crude lathe will produce a perfectly circular piece to fit the hole. Hence, although the cylinder is not at all a versatile shape compared with the rectangular prism, its use became widespread from the earliest times, partly no doubt for magical reasons but also, or soon, for its being economical to make and fit – economical of time rather than effort, for a primitive lathe is no joke to work.

In forming processes the form – for example an anvil – and in casting processes the mould, take the place of the jig as automatic aids to flattening.

Although cutting a surface flat in any material is not inherently an easy job, the invention of jigged and self-jigging tools at least facilitated it; and for the sake of versatility, and thence of avoiding fitting and offering up, and thence of economy, it became a normal procedure in all constructing trades to square the components before putting them together.

Thus the first and most important stratagem adopted to cheapen construction was the squaring and turning of components in order to eliminate offering up and individual fitting. The flatness, straightness and square-ness which more than any other characteristic distinguish man's construction from the works of God, derive from economy. We see the mark of economy in every building of squared masonry however magnificent it may be. Only the few remnants of ancient polygonal masonry remind us that the pattern of stone work where each stone is individually fitted can be very different from the cheap squared pattern to which we are accustomed. Cheap need not be nasty. But it is apparent that for one reason or another the ancients felt stone joints to be a blemish, and did their best to reduce them to hair-lines.

Now the object of squaring is to avoid offering up and fitting. Only those parts of a component which touch others need be squared. The sides and under surface of a beam need not be squared for the sake of the economy, yet from the earliest times we see that this was done, exhibiting the tendency to standardisation which appears in all constructional design.

It is a great convenience to reduce raw material to more or less standard pieces and then to design your construction in terms of those standard pieces. Such are bricks, boards, planks, deals, baulks, rolled steel sections, pieces of cloth, ropes, bolts, steel sheets and plates. These are convenient to the designer because they save

'Determining systems'. Henry Maudslay designed and made the first effective slide-rest and lead-screw, one of the most important of all determining systems and the parent of innumerable others. He made the example shown about the year 1810.
Crown Copyright, Science Museum, London.

him the trouble of shaping each component individually. He need not proceed like a man building a dry-stone wall who has to select every next stone individually to fit an individual place. He proceeds as if his material could only be found in standard squared pieces and as if his construction had to be designed in terms of those pieces even if this means using more material than strictly necessary. Thus in the steel frame of a modern building some of the material is under-stressed. Beams seldom need to be of the same depth throughout their span; but because the engineer sometimes proceeds as if he were confined to parallel rolled steel 'I' sections, he makes the beams of the same depth all along, or most of them. Standardised pieces of material provide the designer with convenient limitations on shape from the start of his job, of the sort which are always welcome, and perhaps necessary, to designers.

Standardised pieces of material must essentially be versatile. A rolled steel angle bar may end up as a fence post, a frame of a boat, part of an agricultural machine, or of a pylon, or of a window. Thus standard pieces will, wherever possible, be squared or turned. Their squareness will show even after they have been adapted to an unsquared construction. Thus a ship's plates show a square profile even after being formed to the compound curve of the ship's side.

Standard pieces tend to be small. They are made as much for the convenience of their producers as of their users. The object of converting or processing a raw material is not only to improve its properties but also to make it manageable in handling.

Before we examine the influence on design of economy in the remaining techniques, in wasting, casting and forming, we must consider skill, and the meaning of that rather vague word in the present discussion.

In cutting a slice of bread, the intended result, say, is a slice half an inch thick of perfectly even thickness. To achieve this result the knife must not only be moved with force enough to divide the bread but must also be constrained by the interplay of our muscles to move in a plane, and a plane which is exactly parallel with the cut surface of the bread. The achieving of that constraint is skill. Achieving the requisite force is not skill. If too little force is used there is no result. Beyond that, the amount of force does not of itself affect the quality of the result. In a bread- or bacon-slicing machine the revolving knife is constrained not by skill but the shape and arrangement of certain components of the system. There is a slide which constrains it to move in a pre-determined plane no matter how it is pushed: a built-in jig. The constraint is mechanical not skilled, constant not variable. The movement of our eyelids is, as it were, mechanically constrained. One cannot bat one's eyelids skilfully.

Any system for making things which requires skilled constraint (exercised by a man or a computer) we shall call a skilled system, while if the constraint is mechanical we shall speak of a shape-determining system or, for short a 'determining-system'.

The criterion by which a determining-system is distinguished from a skilled system is simply the constancy of the constraint. If the shape which the material takes in the result is predetermined, whether by a form or by a mould, or by jigs – components which govern the relative motion of a work-piece and a tool – then the system is a determining system. But any system in which constraint is variable at will is a skilled system. The distinction has nothing to do with the source from which energy comes to work the system. An electrically driven dentist's drill is entirely constrained by skill except in its rotation, and it is a 'hand tool'. But any modern hand-driven drill, once it has started its hole in a piece of wood or metal, is constrained mechanically. You cannot change its direction after that. You have become involved in a determining-system to which you are merely supplying energy. You are no longer performing a 'hand' operation, a skilled operation.

In determining-systems the change by which the intended result is achieved is characteristically, though not invariably, continuous. In skilled systems it is apt to be discontinuous; in other words the intended result is arrived at as a rule only by way of a series of intermediate results. Thus if a piece of wire is being made by hand into a spiral spring, it will be bent, then bent further, then moved, then bent again, and so on; the constraint being altered at each stage. But if the wire is wound onto a rotating cylindrical form, or mandrel, the straight wire changes into a spiral continuously and automatically, the constraint being constant.

A jig, then, or a form, or a mould, provide invariable constraints. Systems in which they occur are determining-systems, not skilled systems. But a system may of course be a complex of a determining and a skilled system. Thus a joiner's plane predetermines the thickness of the shaving but only in part predetermines the flatness of the cut.

The word skill, as I propose to use it, excludes any reference to 'know-how' and indicates simply a particular application of dexterity. The old usage of the word did refer to know-how – 'There is not among us any that can skill to hew timber like unto the Sidonians' – and certainly the modern usage does. I think however that it is necessary to differentiate between skill as the exercising of constraint on movement and 'skill' as know-how, for know-how, in making, is design. Thus according to the terms of this book one should say that anybody has skill enough to build a good dry-stone wall but that few know how to design one, for the placing of the stones is a matter of knowledge and judgement, not of dexterity. In that work the so-called 'skill' is in deciding what shapes and attitudes will be allowable in the stone destined for some particular position, not in recognising a stone which has the shape already in the mind's eye nor in putting it in the envisaged attitude. Any one could do those things. It is making the decisions which is difficult, not the execution of them, whereas in sharpening a gouge, say, anyone can make the correct decision but few can execute it.

A system with skilled constraint, no matter what the source of power, usually gets the intended result rather slowly, partly because the change is apt to be discontinuous and partly because it is easier to maintain the constraint if the energy is put in slowly than if the system is worked at full power. In hand work, power and constraint are apt to be inversely proportional as we all can see when we try to write too fast. In any wasting technique which requires skill one works the more gently as one gets nearer to the finished shape. With a determining-system no such caution is needed. It goes without saying that these systems will usually get their intended result more quickly than a skilled system can. That is why they were brought into use.

Prima facie it will always be cheaper to design for

making with mechanical constraint than with skilled constraint because the working time will be less (computer-control excepted). But the shape-determining systems which give mechanical constraint are themselves expensive and are apt to deteriorate more quickly than a man and his hand tools. Hence the cost of the determining-systems must be spread over many products if they are to be cheaper than the similar products of a skilled system. Since determining-systems predetermine shape the many products will all be identical. There will be quantity production of a standardised product.

Continuous production in large quantities, usually called mass-production, does not of itself imply any restriction on the shape of the product. By resorting to a suitable combination of techniques a determining-system for almost any shape can nowadays be devised. Any shape that skill can make could almost certainly be made by determining-systems. But whether it could be made by them economically is quite another matter. If the market for a product is very large and steady then the quantity produced can be very large, so that the cost of the determining systems is very thinly spread, and they can be exceedingly expensive without seriously affecting the cost of the product. But there is a limit, for the determining systems wear out and have to be replaced after a certain time. Their cost can only be spread over the number of products made in that time.

Skill will be wanted in making almost anything which, like a special determining-system, is made singly and not in quantity. But to make any product cheaply in quantity some determining-systems are required. Thus we revert in a large measure to the problem of making things cheaply one at a time or in small numbers. It is the effect of economy on that kind of making which we have to consider.

Our insistence on economy exercises its influence in the same ways on all kinds of making. Whether in mass-production or in 'hand workmanship', if economy is an influence, then the ways in which it can act are in principle the same. The same courses of action can be taken to economise technique in all kinds of making alike. One course is to use a material which is easily got and easily processed, and therefore cheap.

Another course is to keep down the amount of energy required to do the job by choosing, where other considerations allow, a material which is easily worked. In modern woodworking softwoods are seldom much quicker to machine than hardwoods. In hand working the difference is very noticeable and softwood is distinctly quicker and therefore cheaper for a man to work. But softwood is weaker and therefore its sections may have to be designed larger. Thus economy, by preferring a weaker material, affects the shape of what is designed.

Another course is, when designing for production by skill, to use as little skill as possible. Thus in cheap hand-joinery the fronts of the drawers in a dresser would be connected to the drawer sides by what is called a rabbetted and nailed joint, looking very different from the better dovetailed joint.

Another course, and one invariably taken, is to employ any standard determining-systems which you have already; for instance in joinery a plane or an electrically driven planing machine, a hand saw or an electrically driven circular saw. The trade of joinery, indeed, is wholly based on the use of tools which are standard determining systems for making flat surfaces. Thus in joinery and many other constructing trades flat surfaces and square sections are used in season and out, sometimes where they are needed to make construction easier but nearly as often where they are not.

Half the flat surfaces which one sees in a room are in fact motifs, features of design chosen from among equally useful alternatives; though such is the pervasion of economy that probably no one has been aware that alternatives were feasible. There is nothing natural or inevitable about making the faces of a door flat. Ghiberti's doors in Florence are not so. But flat ones are cheaper.

Another course to take if one wants economy in production, whether of one thing or of a quantity, is to design for an intended result which can be got by one continuous change rather than a series of intermediate results; or if this is impossible, then to design for the smallest possible number of intermediate results, the smallest number of operations. In practice this nearly always limits shape because, although the five kinds of techniques are capable of making almost any conceivable shape they can often do so only by making up for each other's deficiencies. A fairly complicated shape like the body of a small carburettor could be made by carving it out of a solid block of steel or brass using such wasting techniques as boring and milling. A long series of operations would be involved. The same sequence of intermediate results could be achieved, by means of automation, without skill being required, and so the job could be done quickly. But it would be quicker still to make it by diecasting, for this could be done at a single operation. Now this would impose certain limitations on shape. The thing, having been cast in the dies, has to be removed from them, and consequently parts of it must be slightly tapered so that once shifted it will draw out easily. If it seems important to get rid of the tapers then the deficiencies must be made up by a wasting technique to cut them away. But this will not be done. The carburettor will be designed so that the tapers do not matter. The limitation will be accepted. But it will perhaps not be possible to cast certain holes accurately enough, and there the deficiency will be made up by reaming, a wasting technique.

It is through the insistence on reducing the number of operations perhaps more than anything else that economy in first cost influences the shape of things designed. Where there is no mass-production the tendency will be to design a product, or a tool or form to make it, which can be manufactured by one technique unaided. If the technique is a wasting technique then the smallest possible number of cuts will be made and they will be made with standard jigged tools, therefore flat or turned cuts.

One further influence exerted by economy must be noticed. It will always be quicker to make a drawing and to work from a drawing which is made up geometrically, out of straight lines and arcs of circles, for drawing instruments are components of determining systems. There is little doubt that this encourages design in terms of those elements and the tendency is of course strongly supported by the fact that standard determining systems for making squared and turned shapes are so widely available. But in some cases ease of communication as much as anything has prompted the use of, say, a profile made up of arcs of circles rather than a similar but free curve.

In its early days the Modern Movement was in part a reaction against the Victorians' profuse mechanical reproduction of ornamental forms which had originally been developed by freehand skill. The products of industry were held to be cluttered with such ornaments. It was held that machine tools and mechanical processes, i.e. determining-systems, ought not to be used to reproduce forms which originated in hand work, but that *The Machine* should be used so as to evolve its own characteristic forms.

The Machine was much revered. The thing was, to 'exploit to the full the capabilities of The Machine'. That was essential to salvation. The Machine was held to be capable of giving us everything good, at a very cheap price. It was taken for granted that machine tools were manifestations of The Machine. Any machine tools, then, were capable of making things which were good and also cheap.

So they are. But they are much more easily capable of making things which are bad; and hand tools are, if anything, capable of making things which are worse.

Tools are merely components of systems. They are made by men and controlled by men according to their evil or less evil minds. Tools of themselves make nothing, have no capabilities, and produce no forms. (Neither indeed does The Machine, which after all does not exist and so has not much opportunity). If a man is limited or influenced by the capabilities of a machine it is because he has chosen that machine, and not chosen to buy, or design, or have designed, a machine with different capabilities. If he chooses to limit himself to the forms which certain machines are capable of, he may. If I choose to limit myself to the forms which a handsaw, a hammer and a bag of nails are capable of, I may. But I am not entitled to say that those forms are the characteristic forms of The Hand Tool. They are if anything characteristic of The Bad Workman.

Mass-production is capable of making things both cheap and of very good quality, but mass-production does not essentially depend on machine tools or any other sort of tool. It depends upon the size of the market for your product and on how much you can afford to spend on organising manufacture.

The primary concern of all manufacturers is not with making things but with getting rid of them afterwards.

If you know that you can expect to get rid of large numbers of the same thing year in and year out, or at any rate for a good long time, then it may be safe to raise and spend the money needed to arrange for the thing not only to be mass-produced, but mass-produced automatically. Hitherto complete and thorough-paced automation has not been possible largely because of difficulties of controlling operations automatically. Electronics now make it possible. The ideal before what I have loosely called mass-production is that the form and quality of the product shall be pre-determined in every detail before one single thing has yet been made. The ideal is that once production has started the factory staff shall be able to lock the doors and go happily away. To arrange for any approach to automatic production, with the form and quality of the product even moderately predetermined (instead of their being partly determined during production by the skill of the makers) costs a great deal; but to predetermine a good form and quality rather than a bad need not increase the cost disproportionately, and sometimes hardly at all. In general, mass-production allows the designer more freedom of choice than intermediate or hybrid methods.

If you are designing for thorough mass-production there will not be much question of exploiting the capabilities of machines. If the machines you already have will not do what you want, you will scrap them and design some new ones to do it ('you' being of course a whole orchestra of designers). If you are designing for some sort of hybrid production – and most production is still that – then the question arises, 'capabilities of what machine?' The answer may well be, 'of the machine that we have got, and of Tom who sets it up and George who works it; and they could make it do anything you like except talk, if you gave them half a chance. But don't you start them doing anything fancy with it because that is going to cost too much!' In hybrid production it is always cheaper *not* to exploit to the full the capabilities of a machine, and usually cheaper still to use the wrong machine.

6. Invention: analogous results

The poet invents new juxtapositions of words and phrases which convey a new experience. The inventor makes new juxtapositions of things which give new results. Neither the poet's words nor the inventor's things have any remarkable properties of their own. They are everyday words and things. It is the juxtaposition of them which is new.

Before anything is made, a desirable result is likely to have been envisaged. The man who envisages the result may already know of a system or several systems which are capable of giving rise to it, and in that case no further invention is needed. If you say, 'Invent me something which will result in these books and this alarm clock remaining at rest at this level which I will indicate on the wall', I shall at once think of a shelf on brackets, which I remember to have seen giving the same sort of result with the same sort of things before. I shall not be hailed as a great inventor. I have simply had to determine the class to which the specified result belongs and to consider which devices of all those in my memory give rise to results of the same class. But have I really done even that? I doubt it. I have simply envisaged the books up there on the wall, compared the vision with various sights stored in my memory, found one which showed books half way up a wall, noticed that there was a shelf under the books, and concluded that a bookshelf would do now because it was suitable before.

That can be a bad procedure. There may be other systems which are better than the first which turns up in the memory.

The author once set about designing a draining rack. It was for the plates, pot-lids and so forth used by his family while living in a tent. It had therefore to be very small and very light. Because he started by thinking 'I must design a draining rack' instead of considering what kind of result was wanted, his train of thought was conditioned unprofitably. Racks act by supporting. Any instance of a rack which will support plates must have dimensions comfortable with those of the plates, and there is a limit below which its size and therefore its weight cannot be reduced.

After prolonged thought the designer realised his mistake and started to consider what result he wanted, namely, a row of plastic plates edge-on in mid air. He then started to search his memory for results of the same class but not necessarily involving similar objects or, at any rate, objects which were closely similar. Doing this is not as easy as it sounds. Because it was not easy his mind ran to a result involving objects which, if not closely similar, at any rate were suggested by a very obvious association, namely a row of cups hanging on hooks. The unconscious association must have been plates – saucers: saucers – cups. Thus the thought of plates unearthed the memory of cups.

It was then easy to arrive at the required invention, a thin stick carrying a row of thin wire hooks like cup-hooks; for the desired result was by now well in mind, and the objects in it too, the flexible rather soft plastic plates, which being rather soft at once suggested that holes might be cut in their rims. [2]

Designers and their clients seldom formulate their purposes in terms of the desired results, but on the contrary habitually do so in terms of the systems of things which give rise to them. As the example of the dish rack showed, this may be a bad habit; but it will only be bad if some new factor in the situation, such as plates made out of easily drilled plastic, is overlooked. Otherwise the designer's normal habit is mere common sense. If you want to enable someone to sit, it will be idiotic to proceed in the way that students of design are sometimes advised to do, and think out the whole problem from first principles, as though all the people who for the last four thousand years have been making and using chairs were half-wits. Where the problem is old, the old solutions will nearly always be best (unless a new technique has been introduced) because it is inconceivable that all the designers of ten or twenty generations will have been fools.

When a desirable result is envisaged and the memory, being searched, shows no immediate picture like the bookshelf, then the same procedure must be followed as was done with the dish rack. A similar result involving different objects must be sought, in the hope that the device which gave rise to it can be adapted to the objects which are now intended, or that these can be adapted to the device. It is here that our habit of refusing even to name results, and our habit of referring to them by way of mythical actions, and all the habits of mind associated with them and with the idea of 'function', all these help to make our task more

2. In case anyone wants to adopt this important invention let him be warned that in a breeze of wind it makes a noise like a muffled glockenspiel. Take it down at night.

difficult and to inhibit us from discerning analogies between different results; for we are averse from thinking of classes of results, as such, in any case, and have no proper tools to do the thinking with. Invention can only be done deliberately if the inventor can discern similarities between the particular result which he is envisaging and some other actual result which he has seen and stored in his memory (which must of course be well stored so as to give him a wide choice and therefore a better chance). The fact that we habitually visualise particular results is something of a stumbling block too, in its way. We *envisage* or feel the desired result. We see it or feel it, objects and all. Our memories are visual or muscular memories of particular results, not conceptual memories of classes of results. We see or feel in our memories particular results each including a particular system with its particular components and above all with the particular objects which were involved. Out of that lot we have to abstract the class of result, averting our attention from the particular system and objects. This is not easy when one is reviewing the bloodless ghosts of memory.

If an exact classification of devices were made according to a close analysis of the characteristics of their results it would presumably be possible for computers to invent, provided that their memories were full-fed. For all I know they are doing it now. But it may be doubted whether the classification could be subtle enough or the feeding full enough to enable them to spot far-fetched similarities with the same genius which human inventors have sometimes shown. What association gave Watt his centrifugal governor? A merry-go-round? Who is going to feed a computer with merry-go-rounds?

An inventor's power to invent depends on his ability to see analogies between results and, secondarily, on his ability to see them between devices – a thing which is very much easier to do, for the visible schema of a device is the essential principle of arrangement; and we are fairly well habituated to recognising similarities between devices by means of that. It is indeed our normal means of doing so. An example of analogising was quoted in connection with the design of the lever in Chapter 4. When the designer had his brain-storm he saw an analogy with the yuloh which was the antecedent of his doubled lever. He was looking for a combination of results – the fulcrum steadied, the stone abutted to a block on the lever, the lever stiffened at the fulcrum. The association by which the antecedent was fetched up from the memory was partly visual; the yuloh has a step in it, and a lever with a step in it suited the second result of the three desired. But the association was partly by feel, I believe. I had imagined the feel of the lever working, and had once done the same for the yuloh.

It is unfortunately impossible now to discover what trains of thought did in fact lead to the invention of most of our devices, but it is easy to construct hypothetical trains of thought showing the analogies by which they might have been arrived at. For example, we may suppose that a clasp knife was invented in a desire to make a knife short enough to put in one's pocket. A sheath knife was too long. 'How', the inventor asked himself, 'can it be made shorter? How do you make things shorter? What results are shortened results? A telescoped result and a folded result come to mind: Like my footrule'. Here he has found a fruitful analogy, for he envisages a knife folded, handle to blade, like a foot-rule; and the picture in his mind's eye shows him the edge of the blade guarded by the handle – an extra advantage thrown in for nothing. The invention has been made. It remains to improve it by adding a system to keep the knife shut or open.

Such an example may suggest how the process of deliberate invention works. But there is something between deliberate and accidental invention. This takes place when the purpose, the desired result, is inchoate or unconscious. We may suppose that the inventor of the typewriter watched a pianist playing very quickly and thought 'How quickly the notes follow one another. I can scarcely distinguish them. C – B flat – A, could it have been? Letters. If only one could write so fast. Each key writes a letter as you press it. Press. Printing press. Press the key and the little oblong hammer hits the string. Presses the string down. Presses the letter. The letter is printed on the paper.' There he has the typewriter, each hammer in the action of the piano printing its own letter. He saw the analogy between the two results, a sounded letter and a printed letter.[3]

A desired result is not always envisaged before an

3. Some slight colour is given to this story by the fact that early typewriters had piano keys.

invention is made. More commonly perhaps an accident will produce a result which is only then seen to be desirable. Whatever a designer's purpose may be, he ought always to watch for accidental variations of things designed and take advantage of them in the way of appearance or use, if their results suggest anything to him. Many, if not all, scientific discoveries are made by a kind of inspiration fastening on an accident.

The authors of most of the inventions based on accidents are forgotten. There can be little doubt that most of the cardinal inventions were made thus, before history; but there have been recent examples. A circular saw can be used to cut a groove in wood, the groove being as wide as the saw is thick (or a little over, the teeth being set). The saw fits the groove. Some sawyer or millwright made a mistake when he fixed his saw on its spindle. The spindle ought to have been at right angles to the face of the saw, but it was not quite at right angles. He noticed that the groove it cut was slightly over size. This must often have happened. But someone instead of correcting the error was inspired to increase it so that the saw visibly wobbled – in which condition it is called a wobble-saw or drunk-saw – and by this means he made a thin saw cut wide grooves. The width of the groove cut by a drunk-saw is twice the amplitude of the wobble, and it is a most unlikely looking tool, but an effective one.

To take advantage of such a chance occurrence is a considerable creative feat. These things always seem so obvious after the event. An inventor who does this is able to do it because he is able to see not only the particular (and annoying) result under his nose but also the whole class of results which it typifies; and further, because he can envisage the other results of that class in all sorts of different chains of results. He is obviously more likely to make the invention, the discovery, if he has already envisaged such a class of results and desired it before the accident occurs. His mind will then be prepared.

As we have already remarked, there is no essential difference between invention and scientific discovery, for both are the disclosing of a fact about the natural behaviour of things or of combinations of things. Pasteur speaking of scientific discovery said that 'Chance favours the prepared mind.'[4] A classic instance of this was seen

4. Quoted by W.I.Beveridge in *The Art of Scientific Investigation*.

in Fleming's discovery of penicillin. He did not discover penicillin. The action of moulds on bacteria had been observed and reported before he also chanced to observe it. But he had a prepared mind in that he had already envisaged an antiseptic which would be carried in the blood stream, a desirable result never yet attained and one which, to judge from his profession's lack of interest, was very unlikely to be attained. But he believed in its possibility and thought that in the result of penicillin's action on bacteria he perhaps saw a means to that end – as in fact he did. The remarkable part of his achievement was his vision of the end result and persistent search for it. There can be little doubt that most apparently impossible results have been envisaged only after a chance discovery has strongly suggested them and not, as with Fleming, before some apparently trivial accident has led a man of vision to them.

The two commonest sources of chance discovery or invention are play and error. In play one may fiddle about with things aimlessly – or without conscious aim – and suddenly discover an unexpected result, much as one solved the wire puzzles in Christmas crackers by fiddling with them. We shall never know how many of the primary inventions are due to children's play.

In finding by error one may put together a known system in the wrong way, as with the drunk-saw, or make components of the wrong shape through inadequate technique and find that the system gives rise to an unexpected result of which advantage can be taken. If you are bad at building skin boats you may make one unusually box-like and find it unusually stable. You may make another one unusually fine and pointed, and find it unusually fast. And so on.

The man with a vision of some desirable result may deliberately court chance occurrences by experimenting with one thing after another almost at random, as Ehrlich did before he discovered Salvarsan, and Goodyear before he at last discovered how to vulcanise rubber.

We see, then, that finding always precedes design. The finding process may be extremely simple. There is nothing in finding the appropriate system for supporting books against a wall, or for protecting feet. The finding becomes inventive when analogising is involved or that vision which prompts us to take advantage of accidental occurrences. Design as distinct from invention is prescribing a particular instance of the system which has been found, in order to accommodate given objects and a given prime mover; or the combining with this of palliative and other devices. But they also have to be found and their finding may be inventive. Deliberate invention as distinct from design is the finding of a system or a complex of them which will give rise to a desired result, the system or something analogous to it being previously known to the inventor but not previously associated with the particular objects in the desired result (as for example in the case of the dish rack quoted above).

It is certainly very near the truth to say, that if you cannot find any analogy at all with your desired result, then you cannot invent deliberately. If you desire the result of a sky-hook or any other for which no system is known and no analogy can be found, then you can only prepare your mind and wait for something to turn up. And after all, nearly every device we have has grown out of primary discoveries which simply turned up. One might even differentiate invention and discovery by confining the term 'discovery' to inventions arising from chance occurrences not deliberately courted.

There seems no reason, on first consideration, why a system of forces should not first be invented by reasoning from known principles of mechanics, and then clothed in things. But this does not happen. Why should it not? Let us try it. Of all desirable inventions a sky-hook is the most desirable. It would simplify technology quite noticeably. Let us first invent a complete system of forces for a sky-hook and then clothe it in things, and make our fortunes. The problem is to invent it, not design it. A helicopter is a sky-hook of a sort, but somewhat unhandy in the home. We are to invent a sky-hook. The question arises, 'What exactly do we mean by a sky-hook system?' Well, what do we mean? When we know what *things* we mean by a sky-hook system, then, and not before, we shall be in a position to describe the system of forces. Invention must come first.

You cannot proceed by saying, 'Here is the result, thing suspended in mid-air; let us think out how to produce it', unless you make some assumption about what it is suspended from or propped up by. If your assumption proves good, you have made an invention. If you already know that it is practicable you are using an invention which has already been made.

If there had been no inventions there would be no theory of mechanics. Invention came first.

Theory is an aid to variation of inventions, that is to say, to design. A designer who understands the essential principle of arrangement and the response, will be able to reason about his trial variations. This one has the right arrangement but the desired change is not taking place; why? That one has the wrong arrangement, therefore the desired change can never take place and it must be abandoned. But theory is not an aid to invention as such, except in so far as it enriches an inventor's feel for his job, and no one knows how far that can be. Indeed no one knows whether after all a knowledge of theory actually inhibits an inventor's creativity. In time we shall find out. Our entire theoretical knowledge has been founded on abstractions taken from the fruits of inventions made without theory. Whether theory is a vivifying essence which will enliven our inventive faculties, remains to be seen. It is becoming a commonplace that scientific discovery is an art not a science, being a matter of chance favouring the prepared mind; but we do not yet know whether the mind is prepared or stultified by loading the memory with theory. Presumably some minds will be helped by it and some not. We may be improving our powers of design at the expense of our powers of invention. Moreover it is arguable that we have inventions enough already.

Anyone with experience of training designers will confirm that a man who is capable of invention as an artist is commonly capable also of useful invention. Leonardo's exceptional genius in both useful and artistic invention seems to have fostered the idea that he was exceptional also in combining these two talents; but this is not so. The combination is usual rather than exceptional, so usual in fact that one is led to suspect that both are really different expressions of one potentiality.

7. We can wish for impossibilities.
Utility. Improvement. Economy

We can wish for impossibilities. We can wish and imagine ourselves floating in mid-air because we do not experience floating as necessarily accompanied by certain other conditions such as displacement of an equal weight of fluid, but as an event by itself. We are able to imagine any event without its necessarily concomitant events, the other parts of the response. We can imagine a ship steaming at thirty knots along a canal without making any waves because we do not see making way through the water and making waves as inseparable parts of the same manifestation of energy but, as 'cause' and 'effect', separate.

We get experience by attending and we do that in effect by abstracting one thing or event from all those in reach of our perception and then ignoring the rest (see chapter 14: 'perception'). Thus it comes naturally to us to envisage events in isolation. And of course it comes naturally enough to·us to envisage the events we want and to ignore the ones we do not, so that we can wish for a sky-hook and imagine hooking a hook onto thin air without also imagining the necessary concomitant of that event, the hook falling.

When we wish for something impossible we nearly always wish for a possible event, for example hooking onto air, with impossible concomitants, for example not falling down. But not falling down is a perfectly possible event in itself, as a response to a different system, such as a shelf and brackets. We never wish for or imagine impossible events or things. We cannot. We can only frame our wishes in terms of past experience, in other words of the possible.

The trouble with a sky-hook, or a magic carpet, or a perpetual motion machine, is that they involve unknown forms of energy; that is to say, magic. There may possibly be forms of energy yet to be discovered, but it seems fairly probable that the forms required for those devices will not turn up.

Because we can wish for impossibilities we do so, and we also secretly hope that our wishes will come true. It is not easy for us to accept the fact of Nature's truck. The poet may say 'Ne'er the rose without the thorn' but we are going to breed a thornless rose. We are going to get something for nothing! The curse of Adam does not apply to us; we have swapped it for one or two new ones. We have raised our standard of living.

All cynicism apart, it is obviously questionable whether a higher standard of living entails more happiness, but it is not questionable that a higher standard of living gives better opportunities for avoiding unhappiness. Utility has a strangely negative character. We speak of the secret of happiness, for its causes are elusive; but there is no secret about the causes of unhappiness: thirst, hunger, want of sleep, exhaustion, pain, constraint of movement and too great heat and cold, are evils which can effectively prevent happiness. Utility has a negative character, because useful devices are adopted in the main for the sake ultimately of avoiding such evils.

From the fact that deadly injury, pain and exhaustion prevent the fulfilment of the universal wish for happiness, men have always tended to infer that if only life were safe, comfortable and effortless they would be happy. It does not follow. And moreover the essential actions for avoiding evils cannot all be achieved safely, comfortably, and effortlessly. But evidently this inference has largely determined our modern wishes and hence the devices which have been born of them.

The purposes behind our now insensate search for more and more economy by the improvement of devices originated in these two fallacies: that because the parts of a response are seen as separate events they can be separated, and that because hard labour can prevent happiness, the more ease we have the more happiness we shall get. The first of these two is as old as magic and fairy tales, while the other must be older. But to see magic coming true is something new. To all appearances we really have separated the parts of the response, and we have indeed banished hard labour from many lives. And yet we are not quite happy. Happiness is just round the corner, and we shall reach it when we have improved everything a bit more, just a bit more.

Our insatiability is of course carefully tended by the salesmen. They do not want satisfied customers. They want customers who are always expecting some new 'improvement'; and that means something which provides economy on both its levels, cheaper in price when bought and exacting a lower cost in labour, time and trouble when in use. For us no device ever works properly, for we can imagine impossibilities and improbable possibilities as well, such as electric light. Insatiability has its advantages now and then.

The process of improving a device is mainly a process of accretion. What may be called palliating or economising devices are added to or incorporated in the original device to such an extent that the simple foundation of the resulting complex is often difficult to discover.

All that remains after a typewriter has been used – after energy has been put in and has passed through the system – is marked paper. That is the result of the typewriter, and the only parts essential to it are the type-bar ends, the paper, the ribbon and the roller. With those and some laborious care you could type a letter. The rest of the machine is an accretion of subsidiary palliative devices – keys, carriage and all the rest – which give economy, i.e., eliminate labour and care and give speed. Similarly, once you have stretched the warp you can weave with an ordinary needle. The loom is palliative.

Unpalliated devices are caviare to the general. When Orville Wright made the first powered flight in 1903 anyone of sense would have much preferred a bicycle as a means of getting somewhere. Yet the Wrights' aircraft satisfied the requirements of use.

'Utility' might be represented by some such analysis as:

The satisfying of the requirements of use .... 10 parts
The satisfying of the requirements of economy . 90 parts

Palliation directed to the kind of economy we call convenience has gone mad. But this by no means implies that the majority of palliating devices are trivial misuses of ingenuity. Without lubricating and other anti-friction systems, for example, the wear and loss of efficiency in machines would be so huge as to make them quite useless for lack of economy although, like the Wright's first aircraft, just capable of achieving the intended result and therefore demonstrably satisfying the three requirements of use. Utility is not a matter of effectiveness but of acceptable effectiveness.

Adopting an invention, whether it be a new way to a familiar result or to a result never previously realised, is a decisive step. When once it has been taken it remains to be seen whether a good bargain has been made and whether the bargain can be improved by palliative accretions to the invention which reduce the cost of it.

It often happens that one invention supersedes and outlives another not because it achieves any different result but because it is capable of carrying a greater variety of palliative systems, or some particularly desirable palliative system. Thus the ship superseded the raft, which is wet and top-heavy if carrying much freight, and the aircraft superseded the airship, which is slower. Yet the raft is much harder to sink than the ship, and the airship is less liable to fall down than the aircraft.

From these considerations it follows that what we see of a device is rarely the essential part, the *sine qua non,* but nearly always merely the superstructure which economy has imposed on it. Economy, if sufficiently insisted on, can exert a very powerful influence indeed upon the appearance of devices though, since requirements for economy are invariably conflicting, even economy never does in fact govern appearance, as we shall see in the next chapter.

8. The requirements conflict. Compromise

The requirements for design conflict and cannot be reconciled. All designs for devices are in some degree failures, either because they flout one or another of the requirements or because they are compromises, and compromise implies a degree of failure.

Failure is inherent in all useful design not only because all requirements of economy derive from insatiable wishes, but more immediately because certain quite specific conflicts are inevitable once requirements for economy are admitted; and conflicts even among the requirements of use are not unknown.

It follows that all designs for use are arbitrary. The designer or his client has to choose in what degree and where there shall be failure. Thus the shape of all designed things is the product of arbitrary choice. If you vary the terms of your compromise – say, more speed, more heat, less safety, more discomfort, lower first cost – then you vary the shape of the thing designed. It is quite impossible for any design to be 'the logical outcome of the requirements' simply because, the requirements being in conflict, their logical outcome is an impossibility. It must however be remembered that by the use of magic, that is to say by unknown forms of energy (of which electrical energy was recently one) impossibilities can be designed; but now that we have nuclear fission and fusion we may have come to the end of magic.

Of the many inevitable conflicts between the requirements of economy the crudest is that between durability and low first cost. The design of consumer goods according to 'built-in obsolescence' is arbitrary indeed.[5] At other levels there are inevitable conflicts between, high speed and low maintenance, high speed and low first cost, high speed and low running cost; light weight (for say, low fuel consumption) and high strength (for durability and safety); more daylight (through large windows) and more quiet, with even temperature in sunny weather; more cargo capacity and more speed; a keener edge and a lasting edge; and as many more as you like. There is also a special group which arises because all requirements of economy demand, prima facie, a minimum condition of the device; but finding out what the minimum condition actually is will be most expensive so that it will always be cheaper merely to approximate it; but, again, if you approximate it you

5. cf. Vance Packard: *The Waste Makers.*

'The quality of workmanship, a good surface, a neat fit ...' Esso Refinery. *An Esso photograph.*

leave no factor of safety. You therefore, in practice, abandon it altogether. The factor of safety you apply is of course entirely arbitrary and varies according to the country you are practising in.

It will be noticed that most of these conflicts ultimately derive from the nature of a response with its inevitably concomitant, and in most cases unwanted, changes.

In the workmanship of risk, and in intermediate forms between that and the workmanship of certainty[6] a conflict is inevitable between the requirements of economy, as low first cost, and the requirements of appearance; for those qualities of appearance which hitherto have been universally required are the qualities of workmanship: a good surface, a neat fit, a clean job and so on. These are the essential, though unacknowledged, bases of design; but they are largely useless and,

6. See: David Pye: *The Nature and Art of Workmanship.*

Regulator clock by Benjamin Vulliamy, 1780, with outer back plate removed.
Crown Copyright, Science Museum, London

unfortunately, avoidable. Probably few people realise how nastily things can be made and still work well enough. There is still so much good workmanship about that we take it for granted and turn up our noses at the people who take the trouble to produce it.

The requirement of accessibility is capable of giving rise to acute conflicts. One of the designer's most familiar predicaments is to be faced with several things all of which for one reason or another have simply got to be in the same place. The enormous elaboration of modern devices makes this inevitable. They are systems of systems of systems, and they have ancillary, accessory, subsidiary, and every other sort of system combined and compounded with them. In addition the requirement of accessibility is also capable of conflicting with those of economy, use and appearance.

A cargo ship provides a convenient example of conflicts between requirements for economy originating in the nature of a response. If you make a ship bigger it will carry more cargo and make more profit. But it will float deeper and have more surface in contact with the water. Therefore when the ship moves there will be more resistance and friction. Therefore more power will be needed; therefore the engines must be bigger and more fuel must be carried; therefore there will be less room for cargo than the extra size suggests. Moreover the greater power will cost more to produce. Moreover the ship being deeper draughted will be confined to loading and discharging in deep-water harbours. One can see that here there will be room for argument about what will be a profitable size of ship at any given time or place.

Some of the most delicate compromises are required in planning buildings, not only because the objects in the system, the spaces to be enclosed, may themselves be a matter of compromise, but because so often several of them demand the same position. If you want to combine with your enclosure some windows for admitting sunlight you must face the sun. If the site has a narrow frontage towards the sun, not all the rooms can face it. And suppose, as often happens, that the only drains to which you can connect are on the same side as the sun, then either the sinks and w.c.s, which have a poor claim to the sunlight, must be on that side, or you must spend more money on the drains and spend less on something else of more obvious importance. Or again, on the first floor of a house whose size is limited by cost, if you want separate access to each bedroom you may only be able to get it by way of a passage, so that the size of the bedrooms must be further reduced to give room for it.

The conflicting requirements which arise in planning buildings can be far more involved than these. The whole art of planning is compromise. Always the requirements indicate unmistakably that several different parts of the building ought to be in the same place at once.

Conflicting requirements for access are artificially raised by designing 'for the market'. We find for example that a suitcase might always be a little bigger. Now if it is designed to be thicker than usual, one's arm cannot hang vertically when carrying it, and gets painfully tired. Therefore one or both the other dimensions must be increased. Clearly the vertical dimension must be less than the distance from hand to ground. Since you do not know how tall the user will be you design this dimension to suit what is statistically the most probable height of the users. The shorter users will now trip over the thing and the taller ones will wish that better advantage had been taken of their height. But even the size which suits the probable height will be too big to go conveniently onto the luggage rack of a train. But it will fit the boot of some cars. But it will not fit others. And so on.

Here is the familiar problem of the designer for production. Since he does not know who the user will be, he does not know what particular systems the thing will be a component of and therefore he cannot really design it at all. A similar conflict is found in the design of easy chairs. Within limits, the lower they are the more comfortable most people find them, at present. But the lower they are the more difficult do old people find it to get out of them, even to the point where they find it impossible. Here however the decision is all too easily made. Old people do not buy furniture, while young ones do. Therefore industry, which can only live where consumption is active, caters more for the young. It is hard luck to be old. But it is also hard luck to be unemployed.

Designers have occasionally been urged to seek for 'ideal solutions of design problems' or words to the same effect. There can be no ideal solutions, as the preceding pages will perhaps have suggested. Design is not like that. There are, however, occasions when it is possible to determine temporarily what is the best practicable balance between opposing requirements of economy, such as high speed and low fuel consumption. The same kind of thing might be done in the design of a structure such as a viaduct across a stretch of bad ground. If there are many piers to support it there will be many rather expensive foundations. If there are few piers there will be fewer foundations but each will be more expensive because each will carry a greater load; and moreover the spans of the viaduct being longer will be more expensive to erect. But again, one long span may be cheaper in itself than two short ones, or it may not. If the engineer really knew what he would find when he dug the holes for the foundations, and if he really knew what would have happened to wages and the price of steel and concrete by the time the viaduct was building, he would be able to state a true problem here and find out the most economical solution mathematically. But his client would still want something cheaper.

It is said that by the aid of computers we can arrive at the correct solution in such cases with certainty. They are clever, these computers! They are going to show us the cheapest answer. But if they think their clients are going to be satisfied with that, they are not so clever as they think.

The fact that compromise is inevitable in so many kinds of design has led theorists to classify design as a 'Problem-solving activity', as though it were nothing more than that. It is a partial and inadequate view.

Most design problems are essentially similar no matter what the subject of design is, but while the discerning layman understands that in the design of large constructions, a new town or an airport, the problems are overwhelming, he probably does not realise so clearly that there are problems just as pressing and difficult for the designer in the design of almost any trivial product. A bad town will do more harm than a bad toothbrush but the designer of either will experience his job as the necessity to make a series of decisions between alternative courses of action, each affecting the decisions which come after it; and if no life hangs on the outcome of the series of decisions about the toothbrush, the livelihood of several people does. The designer can do harm enough if he does not take care. He cannot shrug off the decisions. He has to take the problem-solving aspect of his job seriously.

There are times when the problems are so intractable that they absorb all the designer's attention and seem to leave him little or no choice about the appearance of what he is to design. He feels that he has been lucky to arrive at even one solution which goes most of the way to meet the requirements and as though no alternative to it were conceivable.

There is, I believe, only one circumstance in which that can ever be nearly true. It is the case where the designer has committed himself beforehand always to choose the cheaper alternative, wherever alternative solutions are feasible. Whether it can ever be right for a designer to commit himself absolutely to such a course is very doubtful because a point will always be reached at which a cheaper alternative can only be found by settling for something worse: something less inherently durable, or less useful, or less safe, or having a less durable finish so that its appearance and perhaps its strength deteriorate more rapidly. The washing machine that embodies parts which are not rust-proofed is a familiar example. There is always a worse way of making a job and it is nearly always cheaper.

Even in this extreme case alternative details or finishes will in reality be available which are equally cheap, so that the designer will still be in a position to make the job look better or worse.

The designer always has more freedom of action than appears at first, and particularly in the matter of detail and finish. That matter is of great importance and the quality of the appearance of anything designed depends very largely on it, as also it does on workmanship, which is the extension of detail and finish down to a scale at which the designer has no power to specify appearance directly. In design as in all art the difference between good and bad may be very slight, yet absolute.

Design is not all a matter of problem-solving, neither is it all a matter of art. It is both. The two parts of it are inseparable, as will be argued in chapter 12.

9. Useless work. Workmanship

There is a difference between useless and ineffectual, no matter what the dictionary says. All the things which can give ordinary life a turn for the better are useless: affection, laughter, flowers, song, seas, mountains, play, poetry, art, and all. But they are not valueless and not ineffectual either.

'Design', to many who practise it, must mean, simply and solely, useless work. Nothing they do is concerned with the requirements of use, economy, and access. Such are graphic designers, designers of printed textiles, of decoration on pottery, wallpapers and similar things. To engineers, designers for industries, architects, and naval architects, 'design' means something quite different; yet in all the things they design useless work is invariably done and sometimes a great deal of it.

There is nothing strange in this. Men and animals too perform an immense number of actions every day which are useless, and we find throughout life the same tendency which we find in design and making. In useful design and making there has from the first been a steady insistence on the doing of useless work. We might perhaps expect that early stone implements at least would have been strictly utilitarian, but it was not so. Even some palaeolithic tools are considered to have been made with better workmanship than was needed to make them get results.[7]

Similarly at the present day it is all but impossible to find a manufacturer who assumes that his customers will rather do without the useless work and save their money. Most of the customers may not set much store by the qualities of appearance given by useless work and may not pretend either to value or understand them, yet they will insist on having them and will expect to pay for them, however debased they may be. The maker will be able to sell nothing if he reduces his prices by omitting as much of the useless work as it is humanly possible to omit.

The idea of purely utilitarian design is apparently a fairly recent and sophisticated one. We all, I suppose, have a fairly clear idea of what it is like. The inside of a warehouse, a latticed steel pylon carrying electric cables, an oil refinery, the scaffolding on a building, the manhole of a drain, a steam boiler, a railway goods truck, the chassis of a motor lorry, are examples of it; whereas a living room and its contents are not. The things we call

7. V. Gordon Childe: *What Happened in History*.

purely utilitarian are things which seem to have been made as economically as is possible consistent with their being efficient, or achieving their intended result.

Now they would not achieve that result any the less effectively if they were made less cheap by doing more useless work on them. A steel lattice pylon carrying electric cables does not carry them any better than a marble column would, or a wooden lattice, but it does so more cheaply in the short or long run.

It seems then that the work we call purely utilitarian is not more useful than its more ornamental counterpart. It is merely more economical.

But not much of 'purely utilitarian' design is as utilitarian as we are apt to think. Plastering a brick wall is utilitarian, for it stops the wind coming through (which it otherwise would do to a surprising degree). But making the plaster smooth is entirely useless. Now the same operation which lays the plaster, if skilfully done, also smooths it; so plastering is part utilitarian and part useless. Any number of operations usually regarded as utilitarian have a similar useless content, which, after all, is the better part of workmanship. It does not really matter if walls are out of plumb, yet some builders still bother to make them plumb without being paid extra.

The only work which is entirely useless is the doing of redundant operations or the adding of redundant components, such as applied ornaments.

It is most desirable that one day an investigation shall be made into what makers have thought about useless work in the past: how far they were aware that it is avoidable, and what reasons they gave for doing it so consistently. The ideas of former days and of primitive peoples about it can decidedly not be inferred from those of our own day. I see no reason to suppose that all those ideas were silly. It may be that we have much to learn from them. I do not believe, as I think Engels suggested of the nineteenth century, that makers exerted avoidable effort only under duress. If they had not been willing to do it, it would not have been done. Why were they willing? It is the ideas of the makers, who as often as not were also the designers, which we need to understand. And how did the idea first emerge that useless work really could be dispensed with entirely and that things could indeed be made 'purely utilitarian'?

The idea of differentiating between the useful and the

ornamental, between the structural and the decorative elements in design, is not altogether a new one.[8] Every workman must always have realised that you could at a pinch knock up something pretty crude and yet serviceable, without thought for its looks and quality, so long as it served your turn. (This is a pretty large assumption; but I think that at a pinch, in real emergency, workmen must always have done so everywhere.) But what no one seems to have supposed until the last century was that you could, and even perhaps ought to, base the whole of life on things knocked up like that or little better. The idea must gradually have become current that what had from time immemorial seemed the obvious, the natural, the unremarked and incontrovertibly right way of making things was perhaps really nothing of the sort. Makers and designers must gradually have come inwardly to believe that half their work had been mere frivolity because it had been avoidable, and because some of it had contributed nothing to the satisfaction of men's material wants. This must have affected them like a conviction of original sin. The idea that utility was the purpose of work overpowered them and seemed unanswerable. From that time on perhaps the artist and workman have been weakened by an inward suspicion that they are supporting a lost cause. They have perhaps half believed that the world could get on very well without the contribution that something in them yet compelled them to make.

Workmanship is very largely useless work and, in the West at least, has seldom been recognised for the art it is. It is never easy to say where workmanship begins and design ends, for the simple reason that workmanship is design. Nine people in ten seriously suppose that the good or bad appearance of things depends on their design alone. Their idea is that the designer puts down his design on paper and gives it to a maker who, simply by following it correctly, produces the result the designer intended. By means of his drawings and specification the designer is supposed to give the maker complete information about what is required.

The supposition is wrong because in practice the information never is complete. Life is too short for us to complete it. Always there must be something left to the maker's discretion. Nowadays we are apt to be conditioned to believe that value rests on quantity rather than

8. c.f. De Zurko: *Origins of Functionalist Theory.*

quality, and so we take it for granted that large or obvious shapes matter more than small or subtle ones and that the total effect of a thing as a work of art depends on the gross shape of it – the sort of shape you can describe in a full-size drawing. We pay no attention to such mere kickshaws as surface quality and fine detail; yet their aggregate effect is very nearly as important. To achieve anything worthy to be called quality you will have to do a good deal more than follow a drawing and specification, whoever made them and however carefully.

There is a good and close parallel in music. The quality of a performance depends on the performers as much as on the score. The performers are said to be interpreting the score, but in fact they are adding intention of their own to those of the composer, recognising that no score in practice can fully express the intentions of a composer, that it can never be more than an indication, a sketch; and *no designer can in practice ever produce more than a sketch* even though his drawing is dimensioned in thousandths of an inch and his specification is as long as your arm. For the matter of that, how very few things can ever be precisely expressed. If designs and scores need interpretation, so do contracts and Acts of Parliament, commands and Holy Writ.

The most noticeable mark of good workmanship is a good surface whether rough or highly finished. It is difficult to over-emphasise the importance of surface quality. We see one thing and only one thing: surface, the frontier of something invisible. No seaman has ever seen a ship. All he has seen is a more or less complete coat of paint. No doubt a ship has been propping it up, but the ship and the paint are not the same thing and no amount of argument will make them so. If he sees the ship in moonlight or in a photograph he will be unable to say anything about its colour and may well be unable to make out the exact shape of it, but he will see the surface, still. In discussions about art much is said of form and colour and little or nothing about surface, yet surface may be visible while neither form nor colour are distinguishable. Something is there to be seen independent of form and colour, and the quality of it is only less important to art than is the gross shape of things. The beauty of anything made of wood depends on surface quality to such an extent that a bad coat of polish will ruin the best of furniture as certainly as pocks and scabs will ruin the most beautiful of faces. In neither case has the shape, or colour even, of the features been perceptibly changed; what is generally called the design has not been altered at all, yet the good design is of no avail against the foul surface.

One simple reason why so little is said of surface quality is that we have nothing to say it with. We lack terms. Our way of talking about surface quality as 'texture' is rather like the ancient Roman way of calling anything bright coloured 'purpureus' on the principle perhaps that any bright colour was much the same as any other, and so a swan could be as 'purple' as an emperor.

Our want of feeling for surface can again be seen in the frequency with which people decorating their houses remark on the difficulty of matching the colour of paint to the colour of cloth or wood, holding the samples in their hand meanwhile – at which distance from the eye the appearance depends on surface quality quite as much as upon colour. The two can never be brought to any sort of similitude until they are placed so far off that their specific surface qualities have been lost to the eye.

Under a microscope, of course, the qualities of a surface will turn out to be qualities of shape, just as the edge of a razor, so it is said, turns out to resemble the coping of a dry stone wall. Although the naked eye is unable to resolve the separate particles, grooves, hillocks, transparent or translucent glazes and whatever else may be revealed by the microscope, yet it is able to discriminate very nicely between the blended effects of these in different kinds of surface.

This sensitivity and the sense of quality in general, belong to the makers particularly, and have come to them not because of making by hand – whatever that may mean! – but because most things can only be made in reach of the hand, and so at a certain distance from the eye. A maker is in the habit of seeing things close to him and looking at them closely. He will be all but incapable of looking at the works of man as though they were so much scenery, as an interior decorator or an exhibition designer might see them. [9]

9. In *The Nature and Art of Workmanship* I have put forward a fairly complete theory of workmanship as it affects appearance. The reader is referred to that book for a fuller discussion of the subject.

'The weather in the space'. Church, Romney Marsh

Architecture is differentiated from engineering and from nearly all other branches of design by the fact that the architect has to act as if no object in the result, except the earth itself, is given. His first preoccupation is neither with how to get the intended result, nor with what kind of result to aim at, but with deciding what the principal objects in the result shall be.

The intended results of building are an improved climate or weather, along with protection for those who enjoy it, and their goods. These results can only be

'The weather in the space' chapel at Ronchamp
designed by Le Corbusier
Photo: René Burri. Copyright Architectural Design

achieved at present by way of an intermediate result,
which is, a limited space enclosed. As soon as someone
invents a way of improving the weather even over
limited spaces without enclosure, the profession of
architecture will change a good deal. But for the present, enclosure of space is a necessary intermediate
result towards improved weather, except in the South
Seas, where shade is enough.

It is not often difficult to design a system of things
which will effectively enclose a limited space, and even

if for one reason or another it does prove difficult, the architect's problem in that is not essentially different from the engineer's. He may indeed consult an engineer to help him solve it. The architect's special preoccupation is first to decide what kinds of spaces shall be enclosed. The spaces enclosed are the objects in the result. The kind of result the architect intends is always the same but each particular result of that kind will involve different objects, for different shaped pieces of space will have to be enclosed. The planning of buildings consists first in deciding what those shapes shall be and then in relating them to each other. It is as though a civil engineer had not only to design a dam but first of all to design the water. In nearly all other fields of design one at least of the main objects is given at the start, but to the architect it is not given.

But of course what the architect is enclosing is not space but a fluid, namely air, which like water takes the shape of what encloses it. Strictly then, after all, one of the objects in the result is given to him as to all other designers. But he must proceed as if he were enclosing something which had first to be delimited and then surrounded at the limits. Space for him is something to be cut and carved into shapes and then built round.

All manner of different considerations will influence an architect's decisions about the shape of the spaces he is to enclose, but the chief of them will always be the probable activities of the people who will enjoy the weather in the space. The people using the furniture in a room and circulating among it will sweep out paths in space which must be accommodated by the room; and those paths together make up the space required for the room. But the space of the room may have been predetermined for other reasons, in which case it will govern the paths. The paths and the space as a rule have to be modified to suit each other. They may of course each have to be modified to suit other things as well. The audience and its movements in a concert hall have to be provided for, but the hall is a component of an acoustic system as well as of an enclosing system. The arrangement necessary to the acoustic system will influence the shape of the space to be enclosed. Compromise is involved here as much as in any other branch of design.

11. 'Function' and fiction

Considering that we use things only in order to get results and that in every useful action we perform we are constantly preoccupied with its result, it is really very odd that we have no names for results as such. When we propose to explain what some device or other is for we do so not by referring to the result which is its *raison d'etre* but by referring to the mode of action by which, so we say, it gets its result, which according to the dictionary means its function. We say it is 'for cutting' or 'for supporting' or some such expression.

Now things, as I hope to have suggested, do not by themselves have any actions or modes of action. Men have modes of action and impute to things what they know about themselves. We think of things anthropomorphically. We say a knife cuts, a drill bores, a piece of glass scrapes. But cutting and scraping can only be differentiated objectively by comparing certain results, or the systems which give rise to them. If I am teaching someone to carve with a sharp tool I may say 'Use it like this and it chops away the waste; use it like that and it skims off a shaving thin as paper; use it so, and it merely scrapes; use it so, and the tool will break near the edge, because it is ground very thin.' What I am trying to do is to explain what result will arise if the system including the bench, the wood, the gouge, and myself, is arranged in this way, and that way, and the other. It is the difference between the results that I am interested in, yet I attempt to explain all this by imputing actions to the tool, as if it were alive and capable of doing things all by itself.

We speak of the mode of action of a thing. Action, considered apart from the thing acting, can only be a matter of force and movement. If there are specifically different modes of action of one thing, such as cutting and scraping, there must be a difference in the forces or the movements involved in each. Take a sharp knife, apply it to a smooth piece of wood as in Fig. 15a. Move it from right to left under a slight downward pressure, and it cuts a thin shaving. Take the same knife and apply it as in Fig. 15b, move it from right to left with the same downward pressure, and it scrapes. The forces in each case may be the same and applied in the same direction, the same amount of force acting vertically and the same amount horizontally. The hand and the knife may move through precisely the same path at the same

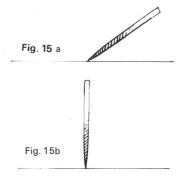

Fig. 15 a

Fig. 15b

speed in the same direction. In (a) there is cutting and in (b) there is scraping, but there is no difference either in force or motion. The point may be demonstrated still more conclusively if a plane is made so that the cutter can be set either vertically or at 45° to the sole. Then if the same plane is used first with one setting and then with the other the downward force in either case may be provided by the unaided weight of the plane. The hand moving the plane will be in precisely the same position in either case, the force applied may obviously be the same if the 'cut' is adjusted carefully, and so may the path through which the edge of the cutter moves.

Now someone may raise an objection to this argument and say, 'You have only considered the recognisable motions and sensible forces. It is obvious that the forces which act at the edge of the tool when it is cutting differ from those which act when it is scraping.' He is quite right. I reply 'Yes. How do you know? Have you measured them?' He replies 'No. But it is obvious. Look at the position of the cutter in each case, and the different shape of the shavings and the worked surface.' He has in fact *inferred the action from the system and the result*. Modes of action always are so inferred. The only way to differentiate the actions in this example would be by instrumental measurement. Moreover we are quite prepared to say two actions are the same when the motions and forces acting are evidently different. In Fig. 16 we should ordinarily say that the wedge was splitting the log whether the force was applied in the direction A or the direction B. Yet at A it is wedging the crack apart while at B it is levering it apart. At A the wedge splits as it moves in; at B it splits as it comes out, turning. We say its mode of action is splitting simply because there is a split to be seen: a result. If different results arise in similar systems, then different forces are involved. True. But we have rarely any direct knowledge of the forces acting. I understand that no one really knows yet exactly what happens at the edge of a cutter and what forces the atoms of it and of the thing cut exert on each other. If so the function of a cutter in fact is unknown. We have no means of distinguishing modes of action as such, and we lump together actions which are quite different. In the case of the wedge just quoted, two actions as different as pulling is from pushing are both given the same name because they give the same

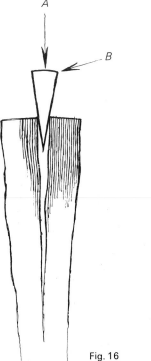

Fig. 16

result – as pulling and pushing may do. We judge by results in fact, though we do not name them.

We differentiate between the modes of our own actions easily enough for we are inside them, so to speak. We do not think about the forces and movements in them and are scarcely conscious of these, very often. We are however well aware of what each action feels like, and that they feel different. The forces and movements may be identical whether your jaw drops in horror or whether it drops to let in a piece of steak. The first mode of action is gaping or gasping and the second is eating. We know whether we are gaping or eating by the sensations and associations and other internal carryings-on which accompany those actions. The difference between the actions is subjective and perfectly clear. There may be no objective difference. When we see someone else opening his mouth we know whether he is gaping or eating by the context of the action. Similarly, when we see a tool moving we know whether it is cutting or scraping by the context of its action, and that is, the system in which the action is taking place and its result.

How else could the teacher of carving have referred to the results in which he was interested? He might have said '. . . it will give a scraped result' or something of that sort, but he could find no noun with which to refer to the result directly, and so he had to impute actions to the tool which he inferred from the result. Here perhaps is the clue to some of the confusion of thought about 'function'.

If we want to arrive at any sort of understanding of the nature of design we must stop vapouring about the mode of action by which a thing serves a purpose and consider the class of system from which an intended result can arise. It is well enough to use the verb 'to function' meaning 'to work', i.e., 'to give rise to the intended result'. But the noun function as mode of action refers to something of which we can seldom have any knowledge.

It may of course be argued that in spite of the dictionary, what function really refers to is the intended result. 'Form follows the intended result' sounds reasonable enough. Now a crane, a lever, and a bottle-jack are all intended to produce the same result and do produce it. So, if form follows function, and if function is the intended result, they all have the same form. If not, why not?

As a matter of fact, 'function of' equals 'result of', or 'what it causes', seems to be approximately the biological and medical usage (though in some instances 'what it causes' is seasoned with a drop of 'how it does it'). Sentences are found such as 'the function of the cerebral cortex is to provide us with . . .' One could hardly substitute 'mode of action' here!

Louis H. Sullivan, who expatiated on form following function in a most entrancing manner ('. . .the form, wave, looks like the function, wave . . .' etc., etc.)[10] quite evidently meant by function something approximating to the Platonic Idea: the eternally existing pattern of which individual things in any class are but imperfect copies. But apparently he did not consider that the copies of it were necessarily imperfect. He considered that the Idea (which he chose to call by the name function) was continually striving to find perfect expression; the Idea being something willed by God, and active on its own account; active moreover through the agency of human invention (in its widest and least restricted sense) so that the form axe might be a perfect expression of the Idea axe for all that it was not a natural form, but man-made.

Sullivan did *not* say that function was the mode of action by which a thing or a system fulfilled its purpose. On the contrary he implied as clearly as possible that it was something altogether different and something mystical which quite transcended such a conception. It is not clear why he used the word function at all. Perhaps the doctrine of functionalism in its received form, took that form simply because the people who read Sullivan naïvely supposed that words have fixed meanings tacked onto them, and supposed that because he wrote the letters f-u-n-c-t-i-o-n he intended the meaning which appears after those letters in a dictionary.

Because there has not been any coherent theory of the nature of design, and because it is evident that what a thing does has some bearing on what it looks like, 'function' has been loosely used to cover any or all the factors which limit the shape of designed things independently of the designers' preference. It has diverted attention from the fact that those influences are many, disparate,

10. Louis H. Sullivan: *Kindergarten Chats and Other Writings;* 'The documents of Modern Art'.

and of various effect, and particularly from the fact that economy, not physics, is always the predominant influence because directly and indirectly it sets the most limits. 'Function' apparently covers economy as well as anything else you please. It is a wonderful hindrance to any understanding of design and will die hard, for it makes a fairly intricate subject look simple.

12. The designer's responsibility

The designer always has freedom of choice. That choice is a central issue. Design is done to get results, but the useless work, the freedom of choice about what the thing designed shall look like, matters as much as getting the result and sometimes even more.

Whatever we do and for whatever purpose, something else matters besides the result we are trying to get and the price we pay for it.

The rightness or wrongness of an action cannot be judged in the conventional way, solely by the immediate effects of it which are measurable, its usefulness or efficiency. The doing of any action and the result of it too affect the state of mind of very many people who were not involved in it, and will contribute something to their hope, or their delight, or their tedium or despair. These side effects are moral criteria also, and in judging an act, such as the act of design, good or bad, they must be taken into account. The side effects matter as well as the intended result. Thus the aesthetics of design are very important.

Social life and civilisation itself, after all, rest on the idea that the manner of doing things is often as important as their result. You do not just chuck some food in front of your guest and leave him to get on with it. But the universality of the idea does not in the least imply that the manner only is important. To insist that every act has side effects and that they may sometimes matter even more than its intended result is not to imply that efficiency is unimportant. It is highly important, nearly always. It is rarely excusable to design and make things which do not work properly, on the grounds that their aesthetic value is more important than their efficiency. What we must do, and insist on, is to have the best of both worlds.

Man's hitherto unswerving devotion to the arts: to 'useless work': is evidence that the importance of something else besides the practical result of making things has always been self-evident – hitherto. It is only in the present age that it has been asserted that 'Architecture is not an art' or 'should not be an art': and that strenuous efforts are made to make a distinction between design and art. And nowadays because we build cities of such a quality that no one likes living in them, everyone who can do so gets a motor car to escape from them. Because of the multitude of motor cars escape is now denied us, the country is destroyed, and the cities become still less tolerable to live in. All that is the consequence of contempt for art. Art is *not* a matter of giving people a little pleasure in their time off. It is in the long run a matter of holding together a civilisation.

Now that technology is rapidly changing the earth's surface and everything which men put on it, design, which includes architecture, has become of more pressing importance than ever before: simply because there is a greater quantity of it and fewer people ever escape from the sight of it. The cumulative effect of design on the human spirit is really important in a simply utilitarian sense. The alien, daunting, inhuman character of modern cities everywhere is communicated to us through the eye. This character may yet prove a more insidious danger to man than any of the poisons he sprays and belches out on the world so freely. It is a cumulative effect, this character. It results from the combined impact of the design of a great many separate things, none of which is so very atrocious but too many of which are flatly negative, wanting. The design of each single thing in the environment, however small it may be, is really important. It may redeem a great deal if it is good, and moreover it may influence other designs for the better.

And yet the question has been raised whether the designer can or ought to be an artist. The contention that he cannot turns of course on the fact that design nearly always involves problem-solving.

No matter how intractable the problems, the designer still has freedom of choice about appearance. To discover and effectively exercise that freedom, however, is not easy. It may involve the rejection of many tentative versions of a design before one is found which satisfies a really exacting sensibility. To make and reject trial versions takes time and that must be paid for either by the designer or his client. Nor does it contribute anything to his client's profit or to the usefulness of the thing to the client's customers, some of whom may well be fairly indifferent to the thing's appearance. In short the designer is not paid to take all this trouble and may not be paid for taking it.

Those who maintain that design is not an art will probably hold that the designer has a duty to the client who pays him and to the people who will use what he

'Outlasts the people for whose use it was made'
Former Monastery S. Maria d'Arrabida, Portugal

has designed but that *qua* designer he is not concerned with the rest of us. In a parallel case the farmer may argue that he has a duty to make a living and produce more and more food for the increasing population, but that here his responsibilities end. But both the designers and the farmers leave their mark on the visible world and more especially, nowadays, the designers; if we take that term to cover all practitioners in all branches of design – engineering, architecture, machinery, tools, domestic equipment and all the other equipment of life. For most of the population, the whole visible scene and setting of their life is the result of workmanship and design.

What is designed and made outlasts the people for

whose profit and whose use it was made. This has always been so and will continue. The fact that a building or some other piece of equipment has been designed to have a life of x years only does nothing to ensure that it will be destroyed at the end of its xth year. Structures intended to be temporary become permanent structures, for the capital needed to replace them does not always come to hand when it ought. Supposing that it did, and supposing that each new generation rebuilt its entire environment so that nobody used anything old, it is very possible that however good the new things were the side effects would be thoroughly bad, for the mental separation of each generation from the one before would be intensified, and on each generation the knowledge would be driven home that everything it did would perish with it: everything it could make would be temporary, and nothing could be handed on, and nothing enduring could be built or done. Inevitably the sense of responsibility that each generation has hitherto felt to those after it, would be weakened or destroyed. It is impossible to believe that this could lead to good.

The things which are made outlast the people for whom they were made and so, in many cases, they ought to. It follows that all designers have a responsibility to the people of the future. But they have a responsibility to far more people in the present than only those whose profit or use they are seeking to provide for. For each man that uses a thing or profits from its making and selling, there will be uncounted others who merely see it and who cannot help seeing it. What anybody sees does something to him.

The scenery most of us live with all our lives was all the work of designers: scenery, I say. We may think we are designing furniture or motor cars, but we are not. If we are designing a motor car for one man, we are designing scenery for fifty thousand others.

Every little thing that goes to make up that scenery is important. It is important in itself, for the beauty of a tree is the beauty of its leaves and branches, but it is important too because each thing we design will influence other designs. Art is not the product of individuals but of traditions, old or new. Every work of art has been influenced by others in some degree.

And let it be repeated, in design, that is to say, in

art, small things matter. The difference between a thing which is beautiful and one which is not may be extremely small. We are all highly sensitive to small differences of appearance. Think of our power of discriminating between the hundreds of faces that we know by sight. Probably the variation in dimension between the features of one or two of them would be of the order of five millimetres. Very small differences matter very much.

No matter how intractable his problem may be, the designer has a responsibility to far more people than those who pay him and those who use what he designs. It is a serious responsibility, and it does not often square with his responsibilities to his clients and their customers. But those responsibilities also are serious. It is folly to pretend either that design is simply a problem-solving activity or to pretend that it is simply an art. It is both. That does not make it easier. The world should not accept designers who are not artists, nor should it those who will not think hard. Both halves of the job need to be taken equally seriously. But for a designer to give due weight and effort to his duties as an artist is often in practice exceedingly difficult and needs exceptional courage and diplomatic skill. The old-style sailor 'was not paid to think'. The modern designer is seldom paid to be an artist. He is paid to solve a problem and probably to help make somebody a profit; and that must always be so no matter how enlightened his client, where industry is competitive.

Design is neither a problem-solving activity nor an art. It is both. All arguments about what designers ought to do seem to be bedevilled by the habit of a mind which thinks 'either. . . .or': *either* all intuition *or* all logic, *either* all artist *or* all problem-solver. This is extremism, and extremism in any cause whatever, good or bad, is evil. Only the man who can recognise in himself the motives of his opponents, however fiercely he may dislike them, is capable of doing good.

In this controversy about design it is to the problem-solver's credit that he understands how masterfully successful a systematic, analytical and strictly rational attack can be in making all the practical decisions involved in design. The journeys to the moon are a sufficient proof of that. He knows that the pressure of population is forcing on us a scale of operations in making the world's equipment which absolutely requires that nothing of importance shall be decided by guesswork any more. He knows that rightly applied his methods can do enormous good. But it is to his discredit if he also believes, not only that men can live by bread alone, but ought to. If so perhaps he is afraid of irrationality: and art, to him, is irrationality. He may have, too, a feeling that the people who set so much store by art share a great secret from which he is excluded, and that they despise him; and yet, at the same time, he will think that art is a frivolous triviality.

It is to the credit of the other party, the artists, that they know that men cannot live by bread alone: that usefulness, convenience, efficiency and comfort do not add up to life and never will: and might add up to something pretty bad if they were all the world could offer. But it is to their discredit if they think inefficiency can be excused by art and that efficiency in design does not matter, and if they despise it: is it nothing to them that they only stay alive through the efficiency of shipping, farming and public services? They sometimes talk as though they were above all that. It is to their discredit, too, if they foster the mystique of art by refusing to think out what they are at.

But many times the two parties to the controversy, the artist and the problem solver, are both together in one skin. Every good designer is made up of both. Nor does he think of art as God and problem-solving as Mammon, but thinks of the two as inseparable parts of one whole, like the mind and body of man, each dependent on the other and each affecting the other. He does not think there is room for both. He knows there is need, absolute necessity for both.

Efficiency, the capability of performing effectively, never made anything beautiful yet and it justifies no design in itself. To say of a design 'it works, it does its job', or 'it gets the intended result' no more commends or excuses it than to say of a man 'he has never actually defrauded anybody'. That is not what virtue means! Something more is required.

If design is a problem-solving activity it is also an art. Let us forget the all too common phrase 'Art and Design' suggesting as it inevitably does that design is distinct from art.

13. The aesthetics of design

There are two questions which concern every designer. First: if some things are of 'good' appearance while others are not, why are the 'good' ones good and the 'bad' ones bad? What causes the difference? Second: supposing that they are good, who is the better for it? Does it really matter? If so, why?

These are questions of aesthetics. Even if we confine that term to the 'philosophy of the perception of beauty' inevitably the second question, the question of value, arises. The questions of the nature of beauty and of its value are intertwined.

Beauty seems a difficult word to use nowadays. It seems to convey a sense of something extreme, the sort of thing that somebody might swoon at; or else if not that, of something suave and pretty. Consequently we find ourselves using circumlocutions and saying 'It looks good' or 'It looks right' or (detestably ambiguous slang!) 'It 'works' ', when we ought to be saying without any sense of extravagance or pretentiousness, 'It is beautiful'. Let us call a beautiful spade a beautiful spade, then. The most unassuming, unpretentious and unemphatic things may be beautiful. Anything in the world may be beautiful and an endless multitude of things in it are beautiful: they 'look right'.

If I were to set out, in the footsteps of Descartes, to doubt everything I could, there would be one certainty at least which I know I should never be able to shake: the world is beautiful. Yet if I say to another man 'That thing there is beautiful' and get the reply 'I do not see it. Explain to me why', then every word of explanation I or anyone may give will be beside the point. No words can ever enable a man to see that something is beautiful. Beauty is something which cannot be pointed out.

Take for example the building in the photograph of The Caol Isla Distillery. I say – in all sincerity – 'There is a fine building, and worthy of its site, too. A beautiful thing'. Suppose that you reply 'I don't see it. I think it is a commonplace looking warehouse. I would rather see the sea and the shore beyond without any warehouse in the way'. Now suppose that I set about explaining why I find the building beautiful. I may talk of its fine directness and simplicity; of the great stretch of the roof's ridge underlining the farther shoreline of the sound and echoing it; of the texture of the slated

Caol Isla distillery

roof, faintly rippled like the sea, even but not smooth, infinitely variegated, set off by the sharp lines of the lead hips and ridge and valley. I may point out the contrast between the surface quality of the roof and that of the lime-whited brick walls; and I might talk of the proportion between the brick piers and the panels between them; and the delightful punctuation of the brick dentil course that runs along the top of each panel – a master stroke, the touch of a true artist. I could go on like this by the hour. Yet no matter how great were my erudition and eloquence and sensitivity, not a word of it all would be to the point: as you, if you know your job as interlocutor, will very easily demonstrate. 'Ah' you will say, 'Now I see. You mean that directness and simplicity give beauty. Buildings that are not direct and simple are not beautiful. Is that it?' 'NO. Santa Maria della Salute is not direct and simple, neither is St Paul's Cathedral for that matter, neither is half the architecture of the world, but it is beautiful. NO'. 'Oh. But the ripples on the roof, now, and the dentils along the top of the wall: you were trying to tell me why the building is beautiful and you picked on them out of all its other features, so I suppose you mean they are beautiful?' 'Well. . . . . . .yes.' 'So as a matter of improving the environment it will help a lot if I slap a few ripples and dentils onto buildings here and there? It will add a bit of beauty to 'em?' 'NO. NEVER. NO. NEVER'. 'What did you mean by all that, then?' 'I didn't mean, of course I didn't mean, that brick dentils are beautiful in themselves. I meant that they and the other features I mentioned all contribute to the beauty of this particular building on this particular site.' 'Yes, I see. You have been pointing out the different things which contribute to the total effect. You haven't said why they do it successfully on this building but wouldn't do it somewhere else. But never mind that. It is not the contributing features I'm interested in, it's the total effect. You evidently see something there that I don't. What is it that you see? Show me. Point it out.' 'I'm afraid you don't understand. I don't see anything you don't see: or rather, nothing meets my eye that doesn't meet yours, and that's perhaps not quite the same thing. But the point is that I *experience* something you don't. What I make of what I see is different from what you make of it'.

To say 'It is beautiful' is a statement not simply about the thing seen, neither is it simply about the seer of it. It is about the effect of the scene on the seer and many others too. The only known verification of such a statement lies not in the fact that what is seen has some particular measurable or definable property (it has none) but in the fact that it causes a particular kind of experience in many people. The effect is beyond doubt. The cause is still unknown, and except so far as poetry can sometimes bring it before our inward eye, it is beyond the reach of verbal description. Almost any direct comment on or description of the beauty of a thing – such, for instance as I attempted for Caol Isla Distillery – could apply just as well to something devoid of beauty.

If some story makes you laugh aloud, then something in it causes the experience which issues in laughter. But can you describe that something to a person who does not think it funny in such a way as to make him see the joke and experience just what you have experienced?

I am tempted almost to say that in matters of beauty it is never worth preaching to anyone but the converted and never worth trying to make converts. I will not stand by that, for it sounds contemptuous of the 'unconverted' and I am far indeed from being so. But the fact remains that all one can do towards teaching the appreciation of beauty is to say to one's friend, one's pupil, 'I should look at that. It seems to me beautiful. Perhaps you may see something in it too. And try looking at this too, and this, and this. . . . .' That is all. But once your friend has seen eye to eye with you, then you can start talking about ripples and dentils and the rest and perhaps be understood; though it will not matter much by then.

A great deal can usefully be taught about art, about the practice of it. But no one can teach art. The artist must find it for himself.

If for the present you do not find this building beautiful, then look elsewhere at something which you do. Why not? Why is it important for A to appreciate exactly what B does? All that matters, if A is to live something like a life, is for A to 'know beauty' somewhere. I am not the arbiter of beauty, nor is anybody else.

It will now be clear why nothing in this book or indeed in any other can be a guide to Design Appreciation. There *is* no guide to design appreciation, for design appreciation is beauty appreciation (if I may be forgiven the expression) and each of us must learn to know beauty for himself just as he learnt for himself to talk and think and love. Once he has learnt, then what a good critic can say takes meaning and may become useful and interesting – as a commentary. It can never, or hardly ever, be a source of primary illumination. That each must find for himself.

The fact that beauty cannot be described and pointed out is a difficult one to accept because our experience of it is so vivid and clear. But it ought not to surprise us, for the fact is that the quality of experience, of any experience, is never directly describable. Half of literature is an attempt to evoke indirectly what is beyond the reach of direct description. The art of writing lies largely in that.

And even if we could describe and define what it is in the appearance of things that causes the experience of beauty, the definition would do nothing to describe the experience. The cause of the taste of a mulberry can no doubt be stated in chemical and medical terms, but that will not tell a person who has never tasted a mulberry what one tastes like. As for describing experience, try describing toothache to someone who has never yet had it! And we use the same word 'ache' to describe the sensation of an abscess on the jaw and of a broken bone. The term is hopelessly inept and the description no description, suggesting similarity where there is none.

As for describing the cause of the experience of beauty, try to describe the song of the nightingale. It is, so I understand, beyond the reach of musical notation, so that one cannot make it known simply by reproducing it and so avoid the need for description. How has it been described then? – 'Jug, jug, jug, tereu' says the poet. 'Jug, jug, jug, jug, swot, swot, swot, swotty' said the London bird-catcher. 'Contio, contio, contio, contio, tzu, tzu, tzu, tzy' said the German naturalist.[11] So *now* you know why the song of the nightingale has so ravished the heart of man and will do till the end of the world! And note that all three descriptions have depended on coining onomatopoeic words specially for the occasion. Ordinary words in their normal dictionary

11. Frank Buckland: Notes on Gilbert White's *Natural History of Selborne*, Macmillan's edition of 1891.

sense will not do. And descriptions of visual art will never rise to the jug-and-swot level, for there can be no onomatopoeic words for nuances of shape and colour.

The taste of a mulberry and the feel of toothache are simple sensations. But the experience of a work of visual art or of a piece of music in their entirety is not a sensation, it is a memory compounded from a long series of sensations, as will be explained in my final chapter. If a single sensation like a taste is indescribable how can we expect to describe sensations compounded?

It need not surprise us, either, that people do not unanimously agree about what is beautiful and what is not, for they do not unanimously agree about anything whatever. There is surely no subject of importance on which everyone agrees, and yet on any subject there will be found quite a large consensus of opinion at least about the main points of it, while among people who have given particular attention to it there will be found a good deal more common ground than they themselves may realise; for they are the very people who will disagree most fiercely about particular points, and they will tend to magnify their differences and belittle their unity. So it is with the estimation of beauty.

Every attempt has failed to isolate and demonstrate some factor which all works of art have in common and which enables them to stir us as deeply as they do. Every demonstration seems, particularly to artists, far wide of the mark. Yet many able people have thought very hard about this. If many diverse objects excite the same kind of experience in their beholder then evidently they have in some sense a common property; but it cannot be defined in words.

We have now to consider the second of the two questions: If a thing is beautiful, does it really matter? Who is the better for it? How?

No one can live a good life in isolation, without the particular relationship to other people which is friendship: a warm appreciation of people *for what they are*, not for what use they are or for what they can do. No one has ever asked of human relationships whether they really matter or asked who is the better for them! We know that it is good to have such a rapport with people and that life is empty without it. But sight and hearing give us access not only to the necessarily small world of people with whom each of us can have close bonds but also to the whole impersonal world out of which our bodies are made and to which all our senses are tuned, with all its people and creatures among whom we shall never know friendship or acquaintance. In short, they give us access to our environment. To find no rapport with that, and not to appreciate that as warmly, simply for what it is, would be a deprivation and an abnormality only less disastrous than to be incapable of love and friendship and human contact.

Our sense of the beautiful in nature and art is our sense of close rapport with our environment, our sense of intimacy with it. Moreover where we find beauty in works of art we find also a more rarefied rapport with the artists who made them, be they alive or dead. Indeed it is through works of art that we have our most immediate, intimate contact with people of former generations, the artists. Art is addressed to all generations and to future generations more than to its own.

The value of beauty, then, is that along with human contact it enables us to break out of the otherwise impregnable spiritual isolation to which every one of us is born and to feel ourselves at home in the world. Beauty and friendship enable us to get outside ourselves and to live as we ought to live, in concord with the world we are part of, and to feel ourselves part of it.

The aim of design is to promote human happiness. But 'design' is the design of devices, and no device, by its objective results, can ever add to human happiness. All it can do objectively is to promote conditions in which happiness becomes practicable. As we have already seen these are conditions of freedom from the primary ills: freedom from cold and heat, hunger, thirst, weariness, pain, constraint of movement, want of sleep, and so on. All these ills are objective states of the person in which all people find it difficult or impossible to achieve a subjective state they can call happiness. In these states they are, all of them alike, imprisoned in themselves.

Since these are objective, physical, measurable states of the organism they are states which the objective results of devices can often reduce. A house or a bed reduces cold, a plough reduces hunger, hospital equipment reduces the causes of pain, and so on. (But one primary ill, mental suffering is a reality beyond the reach of anything the results, though not the art, of useful design can do.) There is some fairly distinct threshold for each of the objective states within which a man is imprisoned and incapable of happiness. Outside it happiness becomes practicable to him.

No sensible discussion of the aim of design is possible unless some exact distinction is drawn between what are man's needs and what are not, what is useful and what is not. The needs of man – as distinct from his desires, wishes, hopes, aspirations, longings – the needs of man are simply to continue his species and to pass these thresholds. Whatever result helps him to pass the thresholds is a useful result and serves his needs. The results of operating tables or of beds are useful. Those of violins or of pictures are not. But they are exceedingly valuable.

Now, as everyone knows, the mere passing of the thresholds, the mere freedom from pain or cold or the rest of them, in itself produces hardly any happiness. It is true that the first relief from these ills produces intense happiness; but it does not last, it is not enough to live on or live for. Not having toothache is no goal for a lifetime. Happiness, however one defines it, is not something negative, a being-without. It is a positive state of the mind, something added to us. And it is a state of the mind, it is subjective. And it does not mean the same thing to all men alike. Warmth and rest mean about the same thing to everyone. Happiness decidedly does not.

In some fields the objective results of the devices not only serve needs but serve them quite well enough already. No conceivable improvement in design would make a domestic bed serve our needs any better. A bed already does all that is *needed*. It might be redesigned so as to be cheaper, easier to make, easier to wash, and so on; but none of these improvements would make it serve needs any more completely. By increasing convenience they would perhaps slightly increase someone's opportunities for happiness but they would do nothing directly to produce the conditions in which alone it is practicable. That is the nature of convenience. It might perhaps be defined as what slightly increases the chance of happiness but contributes nothing to the essential pre-conditions for it, and thus cannot be said to serve need.

The useful element in design and manufacture can help to make happiness practicable but it cannot make happiness. The only way in which design can make directly for happiness is by beautifying the environment and constantly enriching its visible quality: in short, by art. It seems to be difficult for people in our day to accept the fact that the subjective results of design are ultimately as important as any objective ones can usually be and that they are indeed necessary to anything worth calling life. It seems to be difficult for them to accept that art has deep importance and value. I have maintained that the sense of beauty which art supports, like friendship, is necessary to what our fore-fathers would have called the health of the soul – the health of the innermost springs of thought, feeling and action in man: and that without it he is a man cut off. If that is true, and I am unable to doubt it, then the experience of beauty has good consequences. I do not believe that it is possible to prove that its consequences are good but neither do I believe it possible to prove that the consequences, all the consequences, of any other experience whatever are good. I further doubt whether it is possible to prove that all the consequences of any given action are good – not the action of devoting one's life to the making of what is beautiful and not the action of devoting one's life to any social purpose of any kind. Yet such actions may well be right.

We can see that in reality it is an absolute condition of life that we shall make decisions always in ignorance of some facts relevant to them and always in ignorance of some consequences which will flow from them: in other words, that we shall act always in belief and never in full knowledge.

Now unless the thresholds of freedom from the primary ills have been passed there can be no 'health of the soul' at all. Extreme suffering obliterates every other experience. To the man afflicted by it beauty means nothing. His environment has nothing to offer. In face of it, in face of a world full of it, is it justifiable to spend one's life, as an artist, in the attempt to make the environment more beautiful instead of in relieving suffering?

The answer must be that the relief of suffering is not an end in itself, but has a purpose: to make life more worth living for someone. It is not enough to say to a man 'I have fed you, I have helped you, I have set you free and made you a man again' if very soon he is going to think 'What for?' 'What kind of place is this to be a man in?' To be sure, the artist will relieve suffering where he finds it, as we all must, but since he has something to give which at least a great many people deeply need and which only he can give, he should occupy himself with giving it. He may not see himself as an altruist. Neither, for that matter, do many farmers. Yet we should all perish without their work, however they may see themselves or others may see them.

Moreover the artist may possibly have as good a chance to make life more worth living in the long run as many a reliever of suffering has: for it is true, and pertinent, that some of the most devoted and persistent efforts to relieve suffering have been baulked of their purpose in the long run by the unforeseen consequences of their immediate success. Because of the generous impulse of devoted people disease and malnutrition have been fought down and population has enormously multiplied – with the consequence of more hunger, more strife, more strain and suffering and more still to come. An insecticide which was developed to prevent the disease and starvation of men, and has done so too, has ended by poisoning innumerable harmless and useful creatures. A tribe of Australian aborigines, we are told, is now extinct because they were kindly given blankets.[12]

These things, of course, do not mean that it is futile to try to relieve suffering. They imply only, but strongly, that since we have always to act in belief and never in full knowledge, we are never in a position to assert that any action has, *because of its purpose*, unquestionable moral superiority; for we can never foresee all its larger and further consequences, and a tree is known by its fruit, not by its good intentions.

These, then, are the answers to the question whether an artist's vocation is justifiable in a suffering world; and also to the man who says that society is now in a state of crisis: that the crisis must be faced and resolved by some kind of revolution; that to devote oneself to art is simply escapism; that at best art can only be a branch of propaganda; that to play with art now is to fiddle while Rome is burning; that art must be set aside

12. Elspeth Huxley: *Their Shining Eldorado* p. 203.

till society has been reformed and the Good Life can begin.

This is not the place to argue the ethics of revolution, though what has been said above has its bearing on them, but it is the place to say that in a protracted disaster such as a war or the present crisis of over-population and doubt of values, it is essential that art shall somehow continue. If one generation even, were to opt out of cultivating the arts: or even if a majority of its leaders were to: then they would be defrauding their children of their birthright. The art of the past is each new generation's birthright, the whole stretch of it, good, bad and indifferent: and the art of our time will be part of our children's birthright and their childrens'. It is not for us to withhold it. If it is bad it will be there for them to react against and learn a lesson from. If it is good it will add to the common store. We owe our art to the next generation just as much as we owe the relief of suffering to our contemporaries. Each generation, after all, makes a large part of the environment in which the next will grow up, and that will have a deep effect on them. Consider the loss civilisation would have suffered if the arts had ceased in time of war in ancient Greece, in Japan during the civil wars, in mediaeval and modern Europe. Old wars were not less terrible to the people who were overwhelmed by them because populations were smaller. The people were not less appalled by the seeming hopelessness of their situation. War was no less cruel, and the artist was not remote from it. Those wars are long since over but the art of the times when they took place is still alive and we are the beneficiaries.

If throughout history people had resolutely rejected the arts until 'the crisis was over and the good life could begin' then our arts, and with them our civilisation (which could not have existed without the arts) would still be waiting to begin also.

Crisis or no, while there is life there should be hope somewhere, and so long as there is hope there will be art, no matter how appalling the state of the world, or how stupid and well-intentioned the people who preach about the state of it, saying that civilisation must be stopped in order to preserve civilisation.

No one has been able to give an account of the experience of beauty which squares in any way with what it feels like. Nothing else does feel like it. It makes an impression on consciousness which even when it is quite unemphatic, is specific, and different from that which anything else makes. Whenever we encounter beauty we become aware, each time with a sense of shock and pleasure, faint though it may be, that some emptiness in us, not consciously felt but continually present, has been assuaged and fulfilled. We have a sudden high sense of completeness and harmony. The sense of shock, of sheer surprise, is occasioned I fancy by the enigmatic power of ordinary and often very simple things to convey what seems to be a deep meaning, yet one which we find ourselves incapable of expressing. The sense of fulfilment comes because our attention is focussed and returned to a domain of experience which we live in need of and from which our attention strays in the preoccupations of ordinary life. Every work of art seems to tell us that the proper study of mankind is more than man.

Beauty is an escape. If you are imprisoned escape is good. We are all imprisoned by the unremitting pre-occupations and drives of living: we are full of care. To know beauty is to escape from that prison into serenity, if not often and if not for long, still to escape. I do not contend that art is any kind of psycho-therapy. It is not, though one might go melancholy-mad without it. But the experience of beauty tells us that something in us lives on a different plane from that of our preoccupations.

I have argued that the power of design to make for human happiness rests not directly on its useful results, which only serve man's needs and can do no more; but on its power to beautify the environment: on the fact that design is an art, not simply a problem-solving activity and no more. I should therefore wish to emphasise that the beauty which comes of art is not a slight thing, an affair of giving people a little pleasure in their time off. Beauty is not of value simply because it gives pleasure. There are many people who will say that art is trivial or worse. They would say that it is negligible and superficial compared with all that goes to provide the means of life and material well-being, no better than a kind of spare time amusement and not to be compared in importance with technology and industrial production. Moreover there is a whole propaganda for the triviality and frivolity of art. Any serious artist is bound to ask himself in some moment of discouragement whether after all art may not be as silly and precious as the media of modern publicity are pleased to make it seem. When it is seen against the background of a world whose agonies are continually and vividly presented to us, but whose certainties kindnesses and virtues, not being 'news' are hidden; then inevitably the question of its value becomes insistent and demands an answer.

Part of that answer has already been given; and the whole question of taste, novelty, 'originality' and fashion will be examined at length in the next three chapters. Art is certainly not an affair of endless innovation, novelty of any kind at any price.

Beauty is not of value because it gives us pleasure any more than friendship is. To be sure they both do so, but that simple fact cannot imply that they are valuable primarily because of the pleasure they give; for so does success give pleasure, so does a warm bath. So does the thought that tomorrow is Saturday, so does the discovery of a truth, so does escape from danger, so does eating a mutton chop. The primary value of each rests on something other than pleasure, something to which pleasure is an incidental. The primary value of eating chops is that it keeps one alive, not that it gives pleasure in the process.

A work of visual art may convey many things to our intellect. It may tell a story, be a commentary, convey information, persuade us, provoke us to thoughts we never entertained before. All such things are within the province of art, and because works of art have set out to do them and triumphantly succeeded it may be thought that the essence and value of art lies in the fact that it can do them. But this belief is false. A putative work of art may do them all and yet be 'as sounding brass or a tinkling cymbal'.

The value and essence of art is that it makes us know beauty. If a putative work of art fails in that then it fails finally and is no art however much it may inform or persuade or comment. When we see a true work of art the experience of beauty not only illuminates but in some way as it were irradiates and transmutes whatever our intellect apprehends from it so that we become sharply conscious of much that is quite beyond the reach of direct verbal expression. It is in that that the essence and value of art lies, and it is that which moves us deeply and gives us such pleasure or in other cases appals and wrings us. Such are the consequences of the experience of beauty at its intensest pitch.

But visual art may or may not address the intellect, and if being 'abstract' it does not, that need in no way detract from its power and depth and value and importance. Since our present concern is with the aesthetics of design, an abstract art, we shall not need to examine the questions whether art should persuade or inform or comment, as we should if we were discussing representational painting, for example. Design can have no 'subject' or 'content' in the sense that a picture or a poem have them. It is true that certain kinds of device have become symbols – the plough, the scales, the sword and many more. But the symbolism is incidental. It is not fundamental to the device as the content is fundamental to the poem: no content, no poem.

As everyone knows, art is not the main source of beauty. Art has become important because man is a species of animal which very recently has set an elaborate impress of its own upon its environment. But man's species has existed for an immensely longer period, unimaginably longer, in an unmodified natural environment. That unmodified environment was the matrix of all man knows of beauty. All the means of his experience of beauty evolved in it. Now, in the modified artificial environment, art creates an equivalent for that beauty, for it is a need of man's spirit.

I cannot see or accept what has sometimes been maintained, that the beauty of human art and of nature are different in essence: if only because the aesthetic impact of so many human artifacts is quite remarkably similar to that of grown forms in such things as bones, shells and leaves, even when there has been no intention of imitating them.

What we call Nature is everything which has evolved or appeared as a consequence of this planet having an atmosphere. The form of the earth's surface, of the organisms on it, the face of the waters, of the water vapour in the air, all these and the filtered light of the sun by which we see them, make up 'Nature' as we are aware of it. The organisms which have evolved all play their part in modifying the visible scene, maintaining the surface form of the ground or altering it, affecting the climate, affected by the climate and the seasons, and, moreover, making things, making the soil, making coral reefs and chalk hills, making the colour of the sea and the land, making shells and nests and tools. Man is not unique in using tools, nor in making things; but he is unique in that he will use anything and everything that comes to his hand and will make an endless variety of different things, instead of only one stereotyped kind of nest or shell or dam or burrow or web, however intricate and highly organised it may be. Man is a part of nature, dependent on it and perhaps organised in his brain, instincts and capacities no differently from, though more adaptably and capably than, many other animals. It would be surprising, then, if the things men make were of a fundamentally different order, aesthetically, from those which all the other constituents of nature make: the more so that until very recent times – on an evolutionary scale of time – everything he used was taken as he found it or but slightly modified, and everything he made was made from components which he found, not manufactured – as indeed a great many things still are: baskets, cloth, hedges and many more.

All the first antecedents of man's devices were given him by Nature. Every one of his devices is traceable back to something in nature which suggested the first remote and primitive beginnings of its evolution. And every feature in art that man's mind conceives is conceived by a mind that has evolved as a part of nature: that grew out of nature. Just as gravitation has in man's evolution governed the whole construction of his body and the temperature of the atmosphere his metabolism, so the forms given in the natural world have governed the capacity of his mind to invent further forms and to modify those forms during the evolution of his devices. For the evolution of devices is as much a natural process as the evolution of organisms.

We might confine the term art, if we liked, a. to those activities of man, and only those activities, which he consciously intends to produce what is beautiful. We might go farther and add that b. these activities must be wholly under the control of the artist and not merely initiated by him. If we stop at a. we shall be using the term as, probably, it generally is used now; but we shall have to allow that these are not the only activities

'Baskets'.
Fisherman's basket

of man which produce what is beautiful. If we go on to add b. we shall be in considerable difficulties. No one experienced in any kind of workmanship, however expert he may be, will be prepared to agree that the movements of his hand are wholly under his control. We are all pretty experienced in the workmanship of writing our signature. No one could write his signature twice running so that the two examples were indistinguishable even by eye.

There is an element of chance in all art, considerable in some instances, possibly negligible in others. But because art is the work of man, and particularly where it is the work of a man's hand, the element, I think, is necessarily present. There may be nothing of chance about the design of the work but there must be about its execution. It is hard to believe that chance played any part in the design of J. S. Bach's forty-eight preludes and fugues: but before they can be heard they must be played, and I shall make bold to say that when they are played there is some slight element of chance, no matter who is playing them.

There are some qualities of partly uncontrolled workmanship in the brushwork of paintings, in carving and in calligraphy, for instance, which are extremely beautiful and which have certainly been deliberately courted[13]. There are also some classes of work done, we must believe, without any conscious intention of producing what is beautiful which yet do so in a high degree. Moreover some of the best of these, having been produced co-operatively by the work of successive generations must, in their appearance, differ widely by now from what their earlier contributors intended, for all that they provided the indispensable foundation and ground plan of what we see now. I do not know what one should call the landscape of a long cultivated countryside, or the enchanting pattern of lights which shows at night time in a modern city seen from overhead. Are these not works of art? It is scarcely justifiable to say that these things have taken shape by chance. Each part of them has been made as it is by what seemed a deliberate act, and it need not necessarily be assumed to be a matter of chance that the results of many acts of many men over a considerable period of time should harmonise together aesthetically. If we accept that the doctrine of behaviourism is at the least

13. c.f. *The Nature and Art of Workmanship* on 'Free workmanship'.

a half-truth we shall accept that each man's every action has been largely influenced by his heredity history and environment. But each man's history and environment largely depends on the traditions and conditions of society in his time and in the immediately preceding generations. It would follow that whether they wish it or not, the actions of a community are in fact concerted to the extent that they all have the same matrix. Most of our history and environment is dealt out to us by the tradition of the society we are bred in.

'The landscape of a long cultivated countryside'
Love and Chastity; Florentine School 15th century
*Reproduced by courtesy of the Trustees, The National
Gallery, London*

In further considering the aesthetics of design two things we shall have to discuss are the way in which we look at and see anything beautiful, and the very important question of style and taste in design. Before we can do either it will be necessary to consider some facts about seeing and perceiving.

The process in our brain which results in our experiencing the sensation of sight is set in train by an optical system not very dissimilar from that of a camera. The front parts of our eye act as a lens which projects an optical image onto the retina, a screen round the back of it. A dead eye will still project an image. The first stage of the process is not dependent on sentience.

The retina, however, onto which the optical image is projected, is an outgrowth of the brain. If the brain is alive the energy of the light impinging on the retina starts the process we experience as seeing. It is now understood that different cells in the brain respond each to particular characteristics of the image: one, or one group, to a line at such and such an angle to the horizon, another to another angle, another to some other particular characteristic. The different cells select and admit to consciousness different features of the optical image.

Now, the fact that these features are admitted to consciousness does not mean that they are seen, in any ordinary sense of the word. The subject who is conscious of them may have a clear sensation of them which tells him nothing: '. . . Young babies see, but do not know the meaning of what they see, and occasionally from an injury to a certain part of the brain an adult may lose all visual memory and be reduced to the level of an infant. To such a person a teacup is a curiously shaped blob of white or coloured light of unknown use, though if such a person takes the cup in his hands he will at once recognise it, since his tactile memory will help him out. A person born blind, whose sight is restored by operation in adult life, is in the same case, contrary to popular belief. . . . the picture seen is utterly meaningless and therefore unpleasant, and a long period of training, during which the patient must link up touch and sight and work out the relations between them, as a baby does, is necessary before she will be able to walk about with confidence.'[14]

The baby and the person born blind see without

14. I. Mann and A. Pirie: *The Science of Seeing.*

perceiving. Ruskin knew of this. He stated the essential points well (*Elements of Drawing* 1857. First footnote to Letter 1, 'on first practice'.) 'The perception of solid form is entirely a matter of experience. We *see* nothing but flat colours; and it is only by a series of experiments that we find out that a stain of black or grey indicates the dark side of a solid substance . . . . The whole technical power of painting depends on our recovery of what may be called the *innocence of the eye*; that is to say, of a sort of childish perception of these flat stains of colour, merely as such, without consciousness of what they signify, as a blind man would see them if suddenly gifted with sight. . . . Strive, therefore, first of all to convince yourself of this great fact about sight. This, in your hand, which you know by experience and touch to be a book, is to your eye nothing but a patch of white, variously gradated and spotted; . . .'

The difference between the artist's vision and the utilitarian perception of everyday life, which Ruskin emphasises, is the important point, to which the present discussion will lead us.

The baby and the person born blind do not have to learn to see. Sight is given to them. But they do have to learn to perceive. Perception is learnt and learnt slowly. The same, for example, might be said of learning to communicate by language – skill is required for it. Skill is required for perception as for speech. We are largely unaware of the skill we exercise. None of the things we have to learn to perceive are self-evident, or, apparently, instinctively evident. No doubt, however, we have an instinctive aptitude for learning them, and once we have learnt them we cannot easily see as though we had not. People in a state of shock have been known temporarily to lose the ability to perceive, but normally it is difficult if not impossible to see without partially perceiving as well. As Ruskin says, one has to strive, if one is to see with the 'Innocent eye'.

The advantage of perceiving is that we have a better chance of surviving if we can do it than if we cannot. It is strictly utilitarian. The means of doing it have evolved because it has 'survival value'.

We do it by distinguishing signs among all the phenomena: the appearances, sights, which show up when we see. A sign is something which has been sensed and has been understood as referring to something else. "Whenever we 'perceive' what we name a 'chair' we are interpreting a certain group of data (modifications of the sense organs) and treating them as a sign of a referent."[15]

In order to interpret we have to remember. We can only perceive a chair because we have perceived chairs often before and have learnt what the signs of them are: learnt 'what they look like.' Perception depends on memory, and if visual memory is impaired through an injury to the brain, perception ceases though sight is unaffected.

The whole process of perception may be, and usually is, unconscious. Moreover it may be and usually is impossible to describe or define the signs one interprets. What, for instance are the signs of a table? Probably the only signs which could be said to apply to all tables in existence are: a. a more or less flat top. b. this supported or suspended above the ground or floor. c. the height of the top being such that a standing man can see it. These are loose enough definitions! What are the limits of being "more or less flat"? And it is very doubtful whether these really are the signs we use when we recognise a table. Probably we most often recognise such things by noting first the context in which they appear, which tells us what sort of things to expect, and then noticing a few signs which are common not to all the things of the class 'table' but simply to those examples of it which we have oftenest met before: such as a flat top with legs or a pedestal underneath and chairs somewhere in the vicinity.

Once we have made up our minds – no doubt without verbally defining anything – about the signs, our private signs, by which tables can be reliably recognised, we have in us a schema 'a conception of what is common to all members of a class'[16]: a frame of reference to which we can refer any sight and determine to our own satisfaction – unconsciously still, and with incredible rapidity – whether it means table or not.

Now, once that schema is established it becomes a bed of Procrustes: we mutilate the sight to make it conform with the schema. We all know from experience that greenness is one of the signs of grass, so when we see grass we tend to perceive it as green. We tend to perceive each kind of thing in a pre-conceived aspect. Because we perceive grass as green we say we see it

15. C. K. Ogden & I. A. Richards: *The Meaning of Meaning.*

16. *Concise Oxford Dictionary.*

'The signs of a table'
Table, inlaid ivory. Italian early 16th century
Victoria and Albert Museum. Crown Copyright

Table, cedar inlaid ebony and ivory. Portuguese
perhaps from Goa 17th century.
Victoria and Albert Museum. Crown Copyright

to be green. If we looked hard at it, however, we should say 'what kind of green?' 'Is it all as green as that?' 'Is the part in sunlight the same colour as the part in shadow?' But in normal perception we do none of that. We simply say 'That's grass so that's green'. Once again we may quote Ruskin, from the *Elements of Drawing* '. . . and having once come to conclusions touching the significance of certain colours, we always suppose that we *see* what we only know, and have hardly any consciousness of the real aspect of the signs we have learnt to interpret. Very few people have any idea that sunlighted grass is yellow.'

A similar result of our schemata is the basis for the phenomenon of Size Constancy, which perception psychologists have studied. We are told that because of it all the people in a theatre audience 'look the same size': and that a train approaching along a straight railway does not appear to swell in size as it comes nearer. We must believe that perception ordinarily works in that way. We are also told however that children are found to show less constancy than adults, and artists less than other people. If I may speak for myself, I am incapable of experiencing size constancy – when I look at things as an artist. Then the train does swell and the people decidedly do not all look the same size. When I look I see the train and the people rather than perceive them. The size I see is the angular size which the objects subtend at my eye. To be sure I *know* that all the people are about the same size, but that is quite a different matter from what I see. And this I believe is commonplace with anyone who has been taught to draw.

I do not say, however, that I or any other artist see always with the 'innocent eye'. Whenever we look at something we tend to see in that way. But no one spends every waking minute in looking. For most of the time we merely *perceive* in a very cursory way. We take in the fact that the train is arriving and pick up our bag to get in without taking any notice of what the train looks like as it comes. The most summary perception of train-arriving is quite good enough for the purposes of getting to work. We all ignore ninety nine percent of what we see for quite a large part of our life. We refer what we see to the appropriate schema, and if it fits, that is enough. The activity of reading well exemplifies the summariness and astonishing speed of ordinary perception. One reads a considerable number of words in each second, usually without pausing for an instant to distinguish any one particular letter and without any slightest consciousness of the aesthetic quality of the typeface.

The schema, the conception of what is common to all members of a class, the group of signs by which we know that that is an arriving train: is an abstraction. It is something we instantaneously pick out or abstract from the total sight before our eyes and we ignore all the rest of it completely. That is the normal ordinary, utilitarian process of perception. That is why the man fails to notice his wife's new dress. He perceives her, recognises her, acts appropriately, and quite fails to look at her. But she, very properly, regards herself and her dress as one total work of art, something essentially meant to be looked at, not just perceived. For perception means ignoring: not ignoring everything: the man does not ignore his wife, whatever she may think: but ignoring in the first place everything irrelevant to recognition. If we did not perceive in that summary and instantaneous way we should get run over in the street. If we could not ignore we should die. We have to ignore.

Normal perception depends on ignoring, but the appreciation of beauty and the creation, so called, of art, depends on not ignoring. It depends on looking, and proverbially, the more you look the more you see. What you see, in anything beautiful, is not only all the features of it but also all the visible relations between them.

Perceiving, as we know, is essentially the abstraction of signs from the total of what is seen and the ignoring of all the rest. But when we start really to look at anything beautiful we largely forget the signs and pay attention to things we ignored before. In the language of communication theory, first we attended to the signal and disregarded the 'noise': but now it is the signal we ignore and the noise we attend to. Or perhaps we should rather say that when we look at a work of art the noise becomes signal.

Unfortunately the words 'Perceive', 'See', and 'Look At' are, in ordinary speech, practically synonymous. It is well enough to use the word Perceive in a fairly precise and technical sense because now in ordinary speech it is becoming obsolete. But to use the words 'Look At' as implying something distinct from ordinary perception may possibly seem perverse. None the less 'to look at a thing' implies something done attentively: more than a cursory glance: and most perception is decidedly cursory, or if not that, it is done with astonishing speed and adroitness; so that 'to look at' is an expression which can perhaps legitimately be used by way of contrast, and I propose to use it so rather than to write of, say, 'contemplative vision' as contrasted with perception (which is utilitarian vision). 'Contemplative vision' would suggest something esoteric and difficult, but there is nothing esoteric or difficult about looking at the world and finding it beautiful, neither is there about works of art.

A work of art is a thing which is capable of arousing the experience of beauty in people who look at it. If such a thing arouses in us no such experience, that may be because, for some idiosyncratic reason, we are affected by it differently from most other people; but it is more probably because we have not looked hard enough at it, or have not looked at it but merely perceived it. None the less, each man's response to art very obviously differs, according to his temperament, from that of the next. It is idiosyncratic. And moreover, unless we are on our guard, our response will be strongly affected by whatever associations the work brings to our consciousness; so that we may, for example, see nothing in some work simply because it is, in our time, associated with a fashion which has gone 'out', (next chapter). It would be better to look, and to repel from one's mind every association, favourable and unfavourable.

It has been contended sometimes that our response to works of art is entirely learnt and in no way innate; but the questions 'Who did the teaching, then? and how?' have not, I fancy, been much investigated. This contention is very true of our responses to styles and fashions, but it is not true of our response to beauty (next chapter). There are plenty of artists whose upbringing can really have done little or nothing to point out what became the guiding star of their life, and there are others – many others – who have been studiously encouraged to admire works which meant very little to them and against which they reacted. The only teaching which can lead anyone towards the appreciation of beauty is to say 'Look at this. Look at that . . .' but you cannot teach a man what to see when he looks. You can show him a thing and say 'This is beautiful,' but you cannot teach him how to judge whether something else which you have not shown him is beautiful; for the appreciation of beauty is not a matter of judgement but of response. To say 'Things which have the following characteristics are beautiful' is, always an untruth. The characteristics are there but words have no power to describe them.

I do not think it is ever possible to look at a thing without also perceiving it. There is always a 'double take'. But it is certainly possible when looking at a thing to ignore the perception of it, or at least to exclude that from consciousness. Shelley's celebrated lines about the poet state this authoritatively and exactly:

> He will watch from dawn to gloom
> The lake reflected sun illume
> The yellow bees in the ivy-bloom
> Nor heed, nor see, what things they be;
> But from these create he can
> Forms more real than living man . . .
> (Shelley: *Prometheus unbound.*)

He is describing vision with the innocent eye so far as that is actually attainable.

Clearly, no one can deliberately exclude perception to the point of regressing to the state of a very young baby: nor, I think, would anybody wish to, least of all a designer, whose uppermost preoccupation is continually with the three dimensional, solid, shape of things; and to take in that is perception of quite a high order – the baby probably does not achieve it. Some people say they find that on waking from deep sleep they really do see without perceiving, momentarily. But if anyone has been woken from a deep sleep by a piercingly loud and very beautiful tune he will know what a total absence of perception can be like. The form of the melody seizes one with utter amazement. After a great space of time – probably a few seconds by the clock – the bathos of perception supervenes: . . . 'Why, it is *music*!' That, at least, is the innocent ear! The experience haunts one for days afterwards.

It is absolutely unjustifiable to assume that one man

perceives by the same signs as another; or, for that matter, that he experiences the same things as everyone else when he looks at anything. One can verify by experiment that the results of one man's perception are about the same as the next's in fairly straightforward situations, but that is all. And what he experiences we shall never clearly know – unless he is an artist. Then he can tell us. That is what artists do. And because different men have different experiences when they see, they produce different works of art.

If we experience something different from ordinary utilitarian perception when we look at natural or designed things, what is it that we do? We cease to ignore what perception would lead us to ignore: nothing now seems irrelevant, nothing is 'noise'. The schemata of perception no longer govern us. Grass no longer looks green merely because experience has shown us that greenness is to be expected of grass: it looks blue and blue-green, yellow, orange, and every unnameable gradation of hue between them: the harder we look the more subtle and various the gradations we detect. Men no longer look all of about the same size whether they be close or distant. We no longer 'heed what things they be'. We look at them as if we had never seen one before. We pay, not more, but less atention to what they have in common than we do to the singularity and individuality of each one we see. We disregard all that experience has taught us. When we look at a leaf we forget that it is a leaf and see only shape and colour: a very unleaf-like shape too, in some cases. We see what is literally, actually, shown us and not what is conceptually there. We no longer *use* sights as signs, but *see* all there is to be seen. What it all means, what could be said about it all, is disregarded. Nothing we see 'directs our (conscious) thoughts to something else'. But above all we never look at any one feature of the object before us without being aware at the same time of what adjoins the feature and of its relation to all that can be seen along with it. Nothing is seen in isolation from its setting. It is compared first with this then with that and the other. The eye continually compares contrasts and balances each feature of the scene before it with the others and with the scene as a whole.

None the less, behind all this perception goes on, though not consciously, and we know the meaning of what we see. The train of associations which that meaning arouses flits through our mind at some level below consciousness. The meaning and the associations influence the mood in which we look. The poet whom Shelley wrote of paid no heed to the fact that those hovering yellow appearances were bees, and that the light which struck up at them was reflected from a lake. Yet he was aware of all that, and it evoked in him a mood which pervaded his experience of what he looked at. In the poem he would have written, that mood would have been transmitted: indeed in Shelley's poem it is transmitted: as well as the vivid impact of the actual sight he saw. It was formerly usual to call the mood the sentiment of the work of art and to discuss it as distinct from the work's formal qualities, the qualities which are seen when one looks.

For when, in looking at something, one contrasts one shape in it with another, it is the quality of each shape, its formal quality, its singular individuality, its feel, that one compares, not the measurable characteristics of it. The quality and mental feel of a shape is something beyond the reach of description, but something which in experience is sharply distinct, vivid, real. It is felt as immediately as the expression on a face, though far less describably, for we have developed a considerable vocabulary for describing facial expression, but an impossibly meagre one for describing the quality of a shape. One can describe the shape itself precisely, for example if it is three-dimensional by a projected drawing, but not at all its feel and singularity, that which distinguishes it in experience from other similar shapes.

In the final chapter we shall return to the question of what is seen when we look. Before closing this chapter I propose to digress from the main road of its argument to point out that all we perceive, no less than all we see when we look, is something far other than the world which actually exists. If the 'quality of a shape' as we have discussed it seems to anyone a rarefied unsubstantial and extravagant conception, let him reflect that the 'reality' to which we get access by perception is completely an extravaganza too. What we perceive is *not* the world as it exists. The world as it exists consists of atoms and energy. When you perceive the bare end of a live electrical conductor, do you perceive that energy, and death, are in it? Do you perceive its atomic structure? On the contrary, you perceive its surface and no more. But no surface exists. You perceive a surface where no surface exists because there are inherent limitations on the kind of information which any optical system such as our eye can transmit. The percipient eye and the innocent eye both present to our consciousness a picture of something illusory. What we perceive is *not* the world as it actually exists, at all. It is an analogue of that and a very incomplete one. If the case were otherwise atomic physics would be easy. Most of it would be self-evident.

15. Taste and style

Just as chairs are recognisable as chairs, and as things distinct from tables, so Chippendale chairs are recognisable as distinct from Sheraton chairs, and Gothic buildings as distinct from classical ones. Styles or fashions of design are recognisable, and that is the important fact about them. They are known by the process of recognition described in the last chapter, recognised like everything else which we recognise, by means of a *few* characteristics only, which act as signs of an affinity between all the different objects which belong to the same style of design.

But the experience of beauty aroused by works of art is not, as we have seen, aroused merely by a few characteristics sufficient for the purposes of ordinary, cursory, recognition. On the contrary, it comes of looking at the thing and paying attention to all its features and all the visible relations between them. To recognise the style of a design and to appreciate the beauty of it are two quite different things and come of two quite different approaches to it. Thus it is possible, and perhaps not uncommon, for people to be discriminating about styles and fashions while being insensitive to beauty.

The word taste as used nowadays has two distinct meanings. It may mean the appreciation of beauty or it may mean merely the appreciation of style and fashion. In the first case, when we speak of a person's taste we are speaking of his personal preferences among works of art as determined by his individual sensitivity to their beauty. In the second we are speaking of his knowledgeable discrimination between different styles and fashions, that is to say between different kinds of work, and, more particularly, of his preference for one fashion rather than another, one kind rather than another. It is in the latter sense that the word will always be used in this book.

Now, no *kind* of shape, no *kind* of design or *kind* of picture or other work of art can be beautiful. When works of any or every known kind are looked at some will be found beautiful and some not. The fact that all are of the kind known as Romanesque, say, does nothing to guarantee that all of them have merit as works of art. Some do and some do not. Some have more than others.

To be knowledgeable and alert: to be knowing

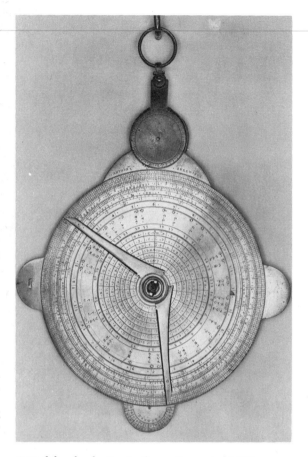

Astrolabe: back. By Anthony Sneewins 1650
Crown copyright Science Museum, London

'The style prevailing at a given time may be of no interest to certain good artists who are working then'

indeed: about fashion and style is an important branch of one-upmanship, which depends largely on being up-to-date and showing that one's taste is only for what is 'in', for what is newest and therefore smartest. To be sensitive to the beauty of things on the other hand avails little if at all in this way, for an appreciation of beauty cuts across all fashions and will often lead the person who has it to cherish things which are out of fashion while ignoring many of the things which are 'in', though worthless as art.

One-upmanship is common enough now and has always been so, but not everyone is afflicted with it. Yet everyone's appreciation of beauty is to some extent influenced by the fashion of his time even though he may regard one-upmanship with all the contempt it deserves. Moreover fashion and taste are not without their value.

No one can be taught what beauty is: everyone finds that out for himself: but he can be taught what are promising places in which to look for it; and taste, as often as not, is what teaches him that. But if taste is sick or degenerate he will be looking in the wrong direction and the chances of his seeing something will be poor: whereas if taste is in health the chances will be good, a tradition will be kept in being, and art will constantly develop and evolve instead of having to make fresh starts first in one direction and then another, as tends to happen at present.

The style prevailing at a given date may be of no interest to certain good artists who are working then. Consequently although there is good art in all times and places, often enough the taste of its own time ignores or underrates it, and later generations are left to discover it, as happened for example to the early work of the painter, John Sell Cotman. The taste, of any group, is conformity, and there is a degree of caution and mediocrity inherent in it. Its effect is the establishment of a canon of works which are 'in' for the group and period in question, and also of works which are 'out': for taste is invariably also distaste. The taste of a given group and period is simply the set of opinions about art which are generally received at the time.[17]

Experimental Psychology as applied to art is, according to the terminology of this book, concerned almost entirely with taste and not with beauty. Such statements

17. e.g. 'Even during the eighteenth century, when every kind of taste was at the lowest possible ebb . . .' J. H. Parker: *An Introduction to the study of Gothic Architecture* (15th ed. 1906).

Nocturnal. Gilt metal. French late 17th century
Crown copyright Science Museum, London

as those given below, for example, are about the taste
of a particular group, which might be an ethnic or a
cultural or an age group: or a group by education or
profession: and at a particular date. The date of any
experiment in this field is one of the most important
facts about it. Modern experimental evidence is not the
only kind of evidence. Taste *does* change with the
passage of time, in any group! Experiments really are
not required to prove that.

Most of the following statements are of types found in reports on experiments on the psychology of 'aesthetics'. All of them, however are statements about the taste of some particular group at some particular period.

'This sort of colour was considered more beautiful than that'

'This sort of colour was preferred to that'

'Such and such a colour looks best against such and such a background'

'A lighter (or darker) colour looks best above (or below) something or other'

'Ellipses were preferred to circles' (or vice versa)

'This kind of line is ugly'

No *kind of* colour – 'a colour': or 'red' – nor any *kind of* picture nor *kind of* anything else is beautiful. Beauty comes always from the singularity of things. Two things which happen to be closely similar in size, colour, insurance value, smell, weight or shape, may both seem equally beautiful. It is not therefore to be deduced that, say, a smell of turpentine is a necessary prerequisite of beauty; and nor is the fact that the two things' shapes are measurably within a millimetre of each other. They might still be as different as chalk and cheese: they might differ hugely in surface quality so that one lived and the other was dead. One judges a man by what he *is*, by his individuality, his idiosyncrasy; not by his measurable properties or measurable behaviour or by the shape of his nose or the description in his passport. So with a work of art.

The argument in this chapter is that the real value, the beauty of any particular work of art, depends always on its 'form', its individuality, singularity, and never on what little it visibly has in common with other works, namely the style it happens to share with them. Taste is concerned with judging works by their style, that is to say by superficial characteristics, and not by their intrinsic qualities by virtue of which alone true works of art continue to have value long after the style they happen to exhibit has ceased to be in vogue and has become a matter of history. Taste, in other words, depends on perception only. You can exercise taste without really looking at anything.

The meaning and importance – a limited importance, as it seems to me – of taste, style and fashion in art particularly need attention at present, for the misconception that they are of primary importance is quite widely held and the art of design seems seldom to be discussed in terms of anything else. Thus it comes about that originality is thought of only in terms of stylistic originality; a question discussed later on.

That an artist should work in the general style of his time is all but inevitable, except in the rare cases of men of exceptional powers who make a fresh departure. The work of the leading users of a still evolving style shows the others in what fields experiment is likely to be productive, and shows them what artifices have been found expressive and may still be capable of further development. This is as much as to say that these works influence the work of other contemporary artists: and indeed there is no work by however exceptional an artist which has not been influenced by the work of his predecessors in some respect or other, however complete the break which he may apparently have made from everything before him. This is eminently true of the arts of design.

It will be argued later on that design without style is an impossibility, and that is a fortunate fact for designers for they would be hard put to it to manage without the restraining influence of a style. The style to which a work belongs is quite irrelevant to its merit, but any style, while it is alive, has a positive value to practitioners none the less, for it puts limits on designers' freedom of choice about the appearance of what they are designing. Adherence to a style as the designer experiences it is simply a predisposition to choose shapes of a certain character and to avoid, particularly to avoid, shapes associated with now demoded styles. If he worked with no such predisposition his freedom of choice would often be limitless and all design would in Lethaby's phrase be 'only one man deep'. But the style gives the designer a point of departure and self-imposed boundaries – ill defined, of course – to the ground he may explore as he makes the series of choices about appearance which, as we have seen, will be forced on him willy-nilly in the process of design. What will concern him, if he is a good artist, will not be merely to 'work in' certain recognisable features and clichés which constitute the style, but to handle such features and to modify them in such a way that while still recognisably

'After the style they exhibit has ceased to be in
vogue' Maudslay's bench lathe and cabinet
Crown copyright Science Museum, London

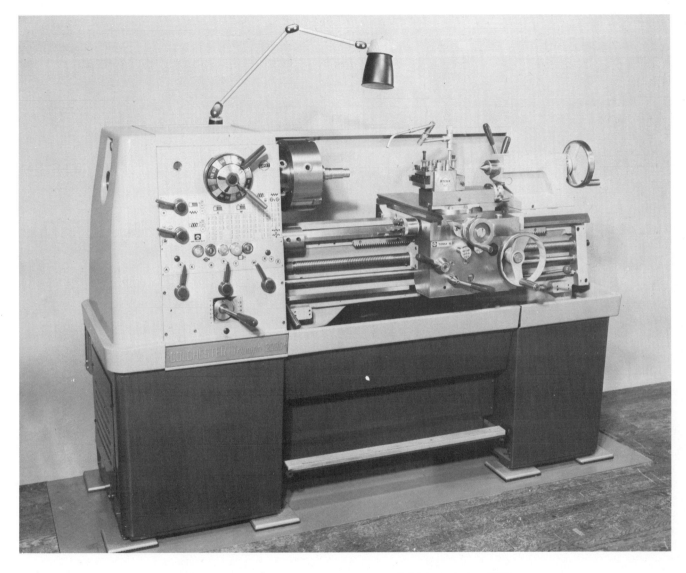

Colchester lathe, 1968
Crown copyright Science Museum, London

prompted by the style they take on a new individuality of their own, and become elements of a work of art instead of a pastiche of the work of the most successful designers of the time; such as anyone can achieve by thumbing through a few magazines.

The making of art is largely a joint contributive enterprise just as the furthering of science is. Each practitioner by his work contributes something to the common stock. In the case of art the common stock is, or ought to be, a tradition which will focus the choices of artists for that time on one comparatively restricted field. Where all designers are working according to one tradition or style a great expertise will develop in making the style variously expressive: in producing an infinity of music out of a limited scale of notes. But this will only happen if the tradition changes continuously and steadily, little by little, and if idiosyncrasies develop here and there within it.

Change is of the essence of tradition. Our declining civilisation has largely lost the conception of tradition as continuous change by small variations – as evolution, in other words – and can produce only fashions which, one after another, appear, live for a little while, and die without issue. At each death another deliberately different fashion is launched and promoted, as sterile as the one before.

The importance of styles is that so long as evolutionary changes in them continue, good design flourishes.

The connection between taste, style and association is interesting. Whenever someone exlaims that a putative work of art is 'horrible' or 'revolting' or flings some such epithet at it, what he usually means even though he may not realise it, is that the work is in a *style* which for him has horrible or revolting associations, and is for him a private symbol. It is this fact which explains a phenomenon that recurs in each generation and by which each generation in its turn seems to be utterly astounded as though it had never happened before. The process is this: The young generation grows up chafing under restraints, or imagined restraints, imposed by the older generation which fathered it, and grows up, of course, in an environment largely made by the older generation. That environment, the whole recognisable style of the older generation, comes inevitably to be associated by the younger generation with the restraints and mental aches of growing up. So, because of that association, once the second generation comes to maturity it turns against the style of the first which symbolises the bondage of its youth. But, by now, the second generation has fathered a third, and when that comes to maturity it rejects the work of the second generation for the same reasons, and also looks back with lively interest to the work of the first generation which its own parents so much detested.

This description is of course over-simplified. Not every member of a rising generation feels repressed, and the work of one generation is never so homogeneous in style; nor is it ever uniformly rejected by the generation after. The work of a real artist will never quite lose all the allegiance it has won, even while the critics are howling it down. The case of Kipling comes to mind. But every artist of our time must be prepared in middle age to face two facts: that the younger generation reject his work, and that the work he himself rejected as a young man is just what the younger generation like. There *is* justice in the world! But 'middle-age' is an over-statement here, for grandmothers of thirty-odd years of age are quite common already. There is comfort in that. We may live to see our work appreciated by our grandchildren.

If a thing bears evident signs of its general style, then once the prevailing taste of the time turns against that style it will become more difficult (though not impossible) for anyone to appreciate the thing's beauty. There was a time not long ago when most people apparently found it all but impossible to believe that anyone could genuinely appreciate Victorian design. At the time of writing the style which was known as "contemporary design" is still out of fashion, but many things of that style too will live; although, as always, most will become no more than "period pieces", the stock-in-trade of future junk shops.

The value of a work of art can only be judged by a generation for whom its style no longer has strong associations. Once that time comes nothing is any longer passionately decried as 'hideous' or 'frightful'. Some things will be seen as funny and many as simply negative, having at best a period charm; while some reputations established earlier will increase and others decrease. But the whole process of reassessment nowadays is liable to be vitiated because new associations of smart fashionableness get slapped on to old styles – a thing we have recently seen in the case of Art Nouveau. Almost any work in that style seemed to get uncritical acceptance in the early 1970's.

Taste influences: slants, indeed: our attitude to everything we look at. As often as it induces us to see geese as swans it makes us see swans as geese. In painting and sculpture the lapse of time is a reliable corrective of these aberrations, though retrospective fashions can reintroduce them in a milder form. But with design, lately, the fact that a thing is old has been taken to be a recommendation in itself, and its merits apart from this verdict of taste are the less likely to be considered.

I do not believe that anything there is, if looked at, and looked at dispassionately, is intrinsically ugly. It may be empty and devoid of beauty, but that is another matter. If we call a thing ugly we do so either because it is in a style against which we are prejudiced (and all of us are so prejudiced in one way or another) or because the thing has unpleasant associations. If we say that a garden slug is ugly we do so because we cannot look at one without thinking of the sensation of touching soft, clammy, slimy things. If we say that a pig or a bulldog is ugly we do so because its facial expression, if we saw it in a man, would disgust and frighten us: we could never find anything good or likeable in the character of a man with that expression; and in addition pigs have always, unjustly, been associated with dirt. If we say that an old boot is ugly we do so because we associate it with what is decripit and sordid: but it is by now a commonplace that when we look at Van Gogh's picture of old boots those associations are transmuted by the beauty of the picture to a sentiment which words cannot express.

The experiences of beauty and ugliness do not necessarily exclude each other. It is possible, as too many people know who have seen explosions in wartime, to experience simultaneously and yet independently, a sense of extreme beauty and stupefying horror. For that matter there are plenty of religious pictures to demonstrate the same thing.

In retrospect the style or fashion in which a thing has been designed is always seen to be irrelevant to its beauty, for in every style we find some designs which are works of art and some which are art manqué. Moreover some things which in retrospect we judge to be well designed appear not to have been influenced at all by the style which was prevailing when they were designed. When they were new they must have seemed to be oddities, and unfashionable.

Because design is so often falsely represented to be a matter only of style and fashion, many designers of the present age have probably dreamt at one time or another of achieving 'Design without style': design where

'Contemporary' chair. David Pye 1950
Wainwright Photo

Chair designed by David Pye 1961
Kellow Pye Photo

'Art Nouveau' Cabinet, veneered, wrought iron
hinges and ornaments
Victoria and Albert Museum. Crown Copyright

'All the quality of appearance that decent workmanship produces'. Sideboard designed by Kaare Klint
By courtesy of Rud. Rasmussens Snedkerier, Copenhagen.

'Aesthetic styling has been completely abandoned': what has been called 'Timeless design': and sometimes (wrongly) 'Anonymous design'.

Anyone who hopes to achieve design without style will, obviously, shun purely stylistic motifs and ornaments and will confine himself to what appears to him the most economically effective form of the device which he is designing. But in vain! Style will emerge.

At any time in history the available technology and the range of inventions already made are capable of yielding far more than they are actually made to give.

'Style emerging where none was intended'. Croft, Barra

Book display table
Kellow Pye Photos.

Bows of fishing boat

Longford cheese factory
Photo: Science Museum, London

Underside of a Surrey waggon
Crown copyright Science Museum, London

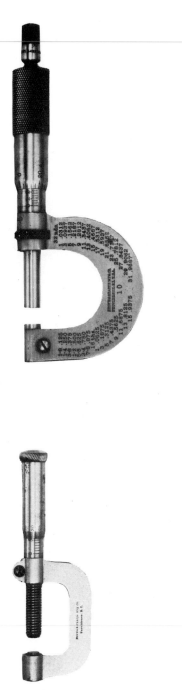

'A style gets seen into them as it were against their will' First 1 in Micrometer Calliper, Brown and Sharpe 1877 (*below*) and by the same firm 1928 (*top*). *Crown copyright Science Museum, London*

There are always innumerable things one could do or make, but which would cost too much. Economy in one or another of its forms governs or influences whatever is done; and in any given technique and time those features of things which are found to be the most economically effective become standardised, or nearly so, and thus come to be regarded as characteristic of things belonging to this particular phase of technology. Because they are seen to be characteristic and standard they act as convenient and obvious signs of affinity between all those things: and because there are signs of an affinity between them we say all those things are of the same style. The affinity we are talking about is a stylistic one. A style gets 'seen into' them, as it were against their will.

When hexagon nuts and hexagon heads superseded the old square ones on bolts, it must have been greater convenience in use which argued for the change: to turn a square nut in an awkward place one may need two different spanners. Convenience here boils down to economy of time and plant. From that time on for many years hexagon bolts were one of the normal features of 'modern engineering'. By means of them alone if by nothing else, any layman of the early nineteenth century could distinguish between one of the new engines and the old ones of Watt's time.

Nearly always when a new feature appears it has earned its place by defeating an older one. Thus wrought iron and cast iron beams superseded timber ones, and later steel beams superseded them; and recently welded compound beams have superseded rivetted ones and rows of rivets begin to be seen no more.

Such innovations of technology were at first seized upon by designers for their economical effectiveness alone, with no thought of style. But soon, very soon, any designer who wished to assert that he was in the forefront of the new movement found it essential to introduce such features in season and out of season, aggressively, and sometimes arrogantly. All too soon they became the symbols of the new movement, the new style. The new-found ability to make a wall all of glass had advantages, undoubtedly, in certain particular cases, but not in nearly so many as the Bauhaus-stylists pretended. It is not forgotten by those who have to work in buildings with these glass walls that their propagators must have known quite well what a green-house was for and what it did. That knowledge counted for nothing beside the imperative necessity of showing how new the 'new architecture' was, by doing something obviously different from the fenestrated walls of the styles which had preceded it.

The earnest seeker after design without style wished for none of this. But he might have expected it. He did not reflect that anything newly invented will in our age at once be used as a symbol of newness: for newness is our obsession. No sooner are space vehicles and space suits invented and designed than a 'space style' based on their economically effective structure and its features appears in the childrens' comics. In the twenties and thirties one still thought of motor cars as having design without style, and of the 'styling' introduced from America as the imposition of a style where none had been before. But as we now see clearly, there *was* style before. Few things have a more powerful period flavour – in other words a more distinct style – than early motor cars and flying machines. The examples of these which Le Corbusier chose to illustrate as 'functional designs' in *Vers Une Architecture* now look delightfully cute.

There has never been any design without style. There has of course been design without obviously stylistic motifs: that is another matter: but never any that could not be unerringly placed by means of signs of style, and could not be imitated stylistically. It is only when a new departure in design is encountered for the first time and unexpectedly that we see design in which we are as yet unable to discern any signs which will enable us to place it. But as soon as we have seen a few more things in the same vein we shall recognise the signs of affinity between them: we shall discern a style.

And in design without stylistic motifs the style can sometimes be extremely unobtrusive. Much Shaker furniture reduced to a minimum the number of features in which a designer's free choice would be bound to declare itself. Yet the character of that furniture is very strong. It could be imitated without making a facsimile and that fact necessarily implies that there is a style to be imitated.

16. Originality

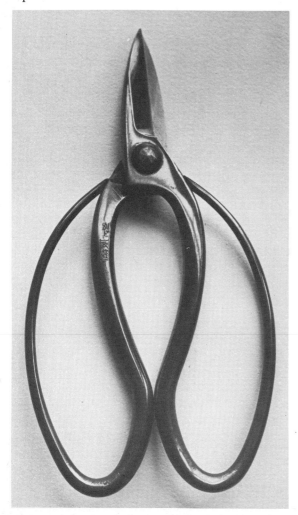

What, in principle, does the artist do? It may be thought that the best way to find out would be to ask him, but that is not so. The so-called creative part of the process of making a work of art is found to require such complete concentration of the mind, even if, as is sometimes the case, the concentration only lasts for quite short periods of time, that one really has very little idea what was going through one's head while one was at it. Considering the remarkable reticence of many better artists, it is a fair guess that they also have been hard put to it to describe what happened. Introspection after the act tells very little indeed.

What I suggest has usually happened is this: the artist has glimpsed something: he has seen, perhaps fleetingly and indistinctly, some particular relation or quality of visible features which had previously been disregarded, and which impressed itself on him by its beauty. By means of making a work of art he then seeks as it were to fix isolate and concentrate what he has seen.

No one has ever succeeded in demonstrating in principle how this is done, but done it is; and when we see it done we find it hard to understand why it should have been so intensely difficult to do. All good works of art look as though they came easily. In a certain way they look obvious.

This account of the 'creation' of a work of art holds that in principle what the artist does is not to create, but to discover, isolate and concentrate.

What the artist discovers, isolates and concentrates, he usually becomes conscious of and expresses in an entirely different context from that in which he first sighted it. A designer designing a tool may give it a profile which derives from something he saw in a mussel shell, or in a turbine blade, or in the lift of a road over some particular hill, or all three; but in nine cases out of ten he will have no idea what was the antecedent or where it came from. It will appear in his mind's eye full grown and full armed, and will come as an inspiration, as if it came from nowhere.

The artist's ability to make his discoveries is perhaps not remarkable. What is remarkable is his ability to isolate them and make them explicit in a transmuted form. It is in that ability, I suggest, and not always in the range and sensitivity of his experience that the artist is remarkable: for if other people were incapable of

'Designing a tool'
Norris shoulder plane

responding to the particular relations and qualities of shapes, colours and surfaces which have stirred the artist then they would fail to respond to the artist's expression of them, albeit in a transmuted form. Probably many people are capable of experiencing, that is to say discovering, most of them, but it is only the artist who has the ability to grasp them, to make them explicit and to fix them: to express what has been experienced. The experience which was fleeting and elusive is caught by the artist, fixed and made repeatable. In the artist's work we see a steady unrippled reflection of our own experience, or rather, of one piece of it. He shows us plainly what we have already glimpsed but failed to grasp fully. But of course the artist's work as he works on it reveals to himself too what he himself has before only glimpsed. It is the hope of that relevation, if not now, then next year or the year after, which impels him to go on working, and which, when achieved, is his reward.

It is an interesting question whether an artist might so attune himself as to find beauty in any and every thing he looked at. I think not. But certainly appreciation can sometimes be highly idiosyncratic. If someone insists that a thing is beautiful which looks empty to all the rest of the world, that need not mean, in spite of

'Originality'?
Cabinet, French c. 1900.
Victoria and Albert Museum, Crown Copyright

what has been said above, that his is a spurious response. Far from it: it may be the response of a markedly original artist; for an artist has to discover beauty in something before he can give it expression and he may sometimes be the first to have discovered it. His expression of it may then make us aware for the first time of something we had too little regarded or had not been fully conscious of, presenting us with something which is quite new to us and yet at the same time disturbingly familiar – *déja vu*.

The natural scene and the made environment which form the setting of our lives all too easily lose some of their aesthetic impact by becoming familiar. We get used to them; and being men we are made so that we have, or we have developed, a need, even a hunger, for what is fresh, unfamiliar, unexpected. We travel to see the world, we hanker to enlarge our experience, we are always seeking some new thing. This hankering, now, is all but inseparable from being man, and in the visual aesthetic field only the artist has power to assuage it.

His work must be unfamiliar – but it must make music too. It will not do for him to make unfamiliar noises of any old kind: of any new kind, rather.

The delight of unfamiliarity, of true originality, is sharpest where the style or convention or general recognisable aspect of the work is perfectly familiar yet is made by a kind of magic to embody something quite fresh and startlingly unexpected. Michaelangelo changed the whole development of painting and sculpture after him but confined his art to showing the naked or draped human body with which Greek artists and their Romanised successors had been occupied for hundreds of years. It is the apparently straightforward unemphatic representational simplicity of some of Corot's landscapes that makes what he put into them, perfectly intangible as it is, so startling. The features of a work of art do not matter for their own sake and may be as familiar as you please. It is the particular relations between them that affect us. The information conveyed by art at all levels may be commonplace so long as the sight is fresh.

This unfamiliarity has nothing to do with crude novelty. Anyone can design things that have never been designed before and write things that have never yet

'Originality'
Avignon by Jean Baptiste Camille Corot
Reproduced by courtesy of the Trustees The National Gallery, London

been written; and for want of art the upshot may well be emptiness and banality. It is a hundred-thousand to one that there has never yet been a page such as you have just read, never in the whole history of the world. I hope it is not empty or banal but I know it is not art for all that it is completely new.

Every individual representative of a species has, besides the general characteristics common to all the other representatives, an idiosyncrasy of his own. No two thumb prints are alike, and so on. This idiosyncrasy will be apparent in the work of a man's hands as much as in the hands themselves. Art, the unexpectedness of art, comes naturally if it comes at all. Art is the imprint of a man: a creature whose nature is idiosyncrasy sparring with conformity. Unless idiosyncrasy holds its own there will not be much art, and it tends to be ironed out when people live in herds. Ersatz, aggressive 'originality' then takes its place.

Originality as generally conceived, so far from being essential, is largely irrelevant to art. The prevalent notion is that the essential business of the artist is to originate new stylistic types, and that any stylistic type which is new must have merit simply because it is so: originality in this sense appeals to taste only.

This misconception has presumably gained currency

'Distinct personal stylistic traits' Chair designed by
C. R. Mackintosh c. 1897
Victoria and Albert Museum, Crown Copyright.

because, particularly in the fine arts, the work of any true artist comes to show distinct personal stylistic traits by which it can easily be 'placed' and distinguished from the work of others. Yet it has long been understood that striving for this sort of originality as an end in itself is the mark of an inferior artist. The personal style of a good artist is never something that has been deliberately cultivated and forced but something that has appeared unsought as inevitably as the personal style of a man's handwriting. But since all artists of note are seen to have a distinct personal style, no artist can hope to make a reputation in a competitive society unless he too can show a distinctive style which easily differentiates his work from that of other artists and draws attention to it. Therefore artists of little capability or uncertain vocation will take great care to make their work look 'different', whereas those with any certainty in them will know that their work cannot help but look different from that of other people any more than their signatures can. It is worth reflecting that the fact of the unmistakable individuality of each man's signature is one foundation of modern commerce everywhere. To establish the individuality of it one need not write it vertically up the page in letters two inches high. And yet there are only twenty six letters, and everyone else uses them too.

Perhaps there is an unacknowledged fear among artists that all the veins have been worked out already and that the mine is exhausted, with nothing left to be won from it. The notion that 'less is more' has led to a *reductio ad absurdum*. 'Where', they ask, 'do we go from here'? The proper metier of the avant garde is to shock the bourgeois, but nothing shocks any bourgeois any more. We can't shock them, so all that is left us is to try to bore and bewilder them by sheer emptiness and monotony. But then we finish by boring ourselves as well. What shall we try next? Come on, we must think up *something*!

If it is safe to say anything about art, it is safe to say that it is not boring. And, conversely, what is boring is not art!

Why should all the resources of design have been exhausted by now, after a mere ten thousand years or less of civilisation? Why after that little flicker of time, a mere three or four hundred generations out of all the aeons of man's evolution? The truth is that too many people are trying to be greater artists than God ever intended them for! The giants who change the whole face of art come very seldom, but ordinary man-sized artists are not rare, and any of them can do something worth doing if he will only find out and accept the limits of his talent: that is the difficult thing. Most of us can only do one or two sorts of thing well enough. But it is the aggregate of the work of ordinary man-sized artists which has made far the larger part of what is best in the environment we have inherited. To be an artist of limited scope is not to be a mediocre artist.

Young designers are sometimes oppressed by a feeling that everything they do looks ordinary. But the fact that it is familiar – to them – and much like many another building or whatever may be in question does not in the least imply that it must be commonplace. It may well have a character as distinctive as their signature, and as their experience grows so the character of their work will become more distinct. It is not until one has been writing it for many years that the individuality of one's signature becomes fully apparent.

Where there is a trade in works of painting and sculpture it is to the dealer's advantage, once an artist has gained a reputation, that the personal style of the work which has made the reputation shall continue; for any work in that style will be easily recognisable as being, say, by the artist X. It will be 'a characteristic X'. It will bear as it were his trade mark, and a customer whose judgement is uncertain and who perhaps wants to own an X simply as an investment, will be all the more likely to buy it. If X decides to make a new departure and starts to explore some different field or effect, and consequently finds that his personal style is altering (to the dismay, no doubt, of the worse sort of dealer), then people who have got used to his earlier style may turn against him: as happened for instance to Turner. But X may find, in our day, that his innovation is quite as unpopular. There is a back-eddy in the current of innovation. The first innovations which were evident in X's style made his name. The name once made, X became an investment. Then the eddy started to turn. For capital appreciation, indisputable, immediately recognisable Xs are required, and the more of them the better. X had better not start anything new.

In the case of design for industry there is a different situation. Here the manufacturer often finds it impossible to maintain his sales unless he can periodically offer a new model which looks distinctively different from those of his competitors. It will seldom happen that he can offer a clear improvement in performance, for technical invention and improvement seldom come for the asking. Consequently his usual resource is to change the appearance of the product, and his designer is constantly under pressure to devise something which looks really different from the model which is to be supplanted. He must do his best to produce a new stylistic type. But it is often difficult to change the stylistic type of a product without sacrificing economy or efficiency. The pressure to innovate generally militates against improvement in either; and where a relatively simple product such as a chair or table is in question it may be a considerable achievement even to maintain economy and efficiency unimpaired when a 'new' design – i.e. a re-design – is made. The best designs have always resulted from an evolutionary process, by making successive slight modifications over a long period of time, not through a feverish insistence on making frequent obvious changes for the sake of offering something which looks 'really new and different'. Innovation often hinders improvement.

17. The common ground between visual art and music.
What we really see

It has often enough been said that all art is one, of the same nature. Yet there appears to be a fundamental difference between music and the literary arts on the one hand and visual art on the other. Music and literature are each a progression extended in time, proceeding from a beginning to an end, while the visual arts impinge on our senses instantaneously. So it seems.

The facts are otherwise. All are a progression, a going on, extended in time. In visual art the progression is far swifter, but the reception of it is just as necessarily a process extended in time as is the reception of music; and as we shall see, the processes in visual art and in music have an essential similarity.

We never do see a work of art or hear a piece of music in its entirety. We can only see or hear part of it at a time. This is perfectly obvious in the case of music but perhaps less so in the case of visual art.

If you fix your eye on something and keep your head still, the whole extent of what you can see is called the visual field. You can only see sharply that small part of it on which your eye is fixed. That part is called the central field and all the rest of it is called the peripheral field. Your vision is at its most acute only near the middle point of the central field. That point of fully acute vision corresponds with a minute part of the eye's retina called the *Fovea Centralis*.

What concerns us here is that the central field, on which your eye is fixed and where alone vision is sharp, is very small: somewhere about a degree across, about what is covered by your first finger nail when you point your finger at arm's length; and you vision is at its very sharpest only round the middle of that. Your area of sharpest vision really is small. Usually when you are talking to someone you can only see one of his eyes properly at a time. If you look at one horn of the moon you cannot see the other with full acuity.

The reader can demonstrate this for himself by putting his finger in the middle of a page of print, closing one eye, staring fixedly at the centre of his nail, and noting how many letters on each side of it are legible. It will be found that they are few if any; but first of all it will be found that staring fixedly at your nail while trying to read out of the corner of your eye is extremely difficult. For all that you can do your eye will keep straying to what you are trying to read, and so spoiling the experiment. From this we learn that the field of central vision is minute, and that once we start to pay attention to any thing in the peripheral field, we automatically shift the eye's line of sight so as to bring that thing to the central field so that we can see it sharply.

One's peripheral field is not blurred only because it is not sharp. It is deficient as well. Various characteristics of things in it are not registered. The sensation of unfocussed vision is different, as anyone with short sight can confirm for himself by taking off his spectacles. As to what is left out of the peripheral view: if you hold your arm out in line with your shoulder and look straight ahead of you, your arm is pointing at roughly 90° to your line of sight. If you wave your fingers about you will probably see them, but if you keep them still you may well find it difficult to decide whether you can see them or not. At about 90° to the line of sight movement is seen well but little else. Now stand a few feet in front of a shelf of books, keep your line of sight straight ahead of you by fixing your eye on one particular book, extend your arm at 30° to that line and guess the colour of the book your finger is pointing at. If your eye is like the writer's you will only be able to distinguish the brightest colours, and those badly; but you will still be able to distinguish marked differences of lightness and darkness and of orientation several degrees farther from the line of sight.

It is impossible to describe the quality of what we see in the peripheral field, 'out of the corner of the eye', in terms of the quality of the central field where vision is distinct. No drawing or photograph can show or even remotely suggest the quality of it. The quality of its blurring is not that of an out-of-focus image, yet decidedly it is blurred in the sense of not being sharp. Apparently it contrives to omit whatever forms the basis of signs of number and colour, and yet it is experienced as continuous, not gappy, in spite of the omissions. And, yet again, although much of the peripheral field is monochromatic (of what colour?) we are quite unaware of this. The most remarkable thing about the quality of the peripheral field is that we are scarcely aware of it, scarcely aware even that there is such a thing.

It is of course possible to determine experimentally

what information one can pick up in the peripheral field at what angle to the line of sight, and so to measure one's powers of perception there, but for most of our present purposes such information about perception is irrelevant. What we experience aesthetically is not quantities of information but a quality, a continuum. And the experimental method is incapable of examining the principal fact of human life, that is to say the *quality* of consciousness, the quality of experience, *what it feels like* inside your head and mine from moment to moment of our waking life.

One is not aware how small the central field is, because, besides making small jerking movements of the line of sight quite automatically while the eye is supposedly fixed, one also moves the line of sight, normally, so that it flits with extreme rapidity from point to point in the scene before it. Thus one is superimposing on a very sketchy general impression of the scene a succession of detailed vignettes in full colour of one group of features after another.

In the central field, because we see more acutely, we see more features than we do in any equal area of the peripheral field; a feature being defined for present purposes as any part or characteristic of a scene which our best vision can distinguish from another. Every feature which we see sharply is seen against the context of the indistinct peripheral field surrounding it.

In comparing music with visual art we may say that in music the 'features' are the notes which are actually sounding, while the context for them, corresponding to the peripheral field, is the memory of all the notes which have already sounded and died away. There would be no music if one instantly forgot each note as soon as it ceased to sound. Neither would there be any visual art if we could see only the sharp central field without its context, the peripheral field: a fact we shall shortly discuss. I suggest that the experience of beauty whether in music or in visual art does not come directly from our sensations, aural or visual, and often owes nothing to any perceptions which may accompany them, but that it comes from something indescribable in the relation or tension between a sharp, vivid, sensation – the note actually sounding or the acute vision of the fovea – and its more tempered context, the remembered preceding notes or the indistinct peripheral field.

Suppose that you look round you and your glance is attracted to some particular thing: a tool, a clock, a picture, a telephone or whatever it may be. Then (1) at the instant your glance lights on it you perceive what it is, where it is, what general shape and colour it has, and so on; and you simultaneously feel, perhaps, 'That is worth looking at'. (2) You take it in your hand, keep your eye on it and your first general impression of its appearance becomes more exact. You notice things about its appearance which you did not take in at first glance. And then, (3), you begin really to look at it, in the way discussed in chapter 14, and the sense of its beauty which was fleetingly aroused at (1) and confirmed at (2) becomes strong and absorbing.

Now, at stage (1), when your glance 'lights on' the thing, your glance, the line of sight of your eye, darts to and fro over the thing with the utmost rapidity, so that within one second nearly all parts of the thing will have been seen fleetingly with full acuity by the *fovea*. And this cursory examination alone will have been sufficient for most of the purposes of perception. At stage (2) your line of sight continues to play to and fro about the thing with the same rapidity, and the first impression gained at (1) is reinforced by the eye's repeatedly revisiting each part. At stage (2) one is apt to believe that one is really taking in the whole appearance of the thing at once, 'seeing it steadily and seeing it whole'. But it is easy to disprove this. Shut your eyes and try to visualise completely what you have just seen. Unless you are one of those rare people who have eidetic vision, you will fail. The image in your mind's eye will be sketchy and full of gaps. It will not be until stage (3) that you will really see it. At stage (3) your eye *dwells* on each feature of the thing in turn. Your line of sight is fixed, and dwells, first on this feature and then on that, while simultaneously and with deliberate intent, you remain aware of all those parts of the thing which are at each moment in the eye's peripheral field, indistinct though they be. This is the process called drawing with the eye, and it is the process of contemplative vision which alone can show us the beauty of the visible world, so it seems to me. To learn to draw with the eye, (and still more, with the hand,) is to unlearn most of perception for the time being and to learn to see instead. I think it is very possible that in many people the sense of beauty is impoverished because they have not learnt to draw with the eye. Possibly they go no farther than the stage (2) we have described.

The succession of acutely seen features causes no experience of beauty unless their context, the peripheral field, is visible. This can be shown by an experiment which eliminates most of the peripheral field. The procedure is as follows: – take a pin and push it through the middle of a piece of dark coloured opaque paper about the size of an open paper-back book. Let the shank of the pin, not only the point go through. If you shut one eye and hold the hole close to the other you will see a field of several degrees, much larger than your central field, as you can tell by the fact that if you fix your line of sight at one side of the hole, things at the other edge of it will be seen imperfectly. But now put the hole six inches or so in front of your eye and look through it at something fairly close to you and against the light. A plant standing in the window will do very well. Now the hole will take in very little beyond the central field. The field will look minute. Now try to get a sense of the shape and beauty of the plant by moving your pinhole-field all over it. Having practised that, get a book of large reproductions of pictures, get someone to open it where you cannot see it, and let them put it about a foot from you in a very strong light so that you can look at it in the same way. It will probably be some time before you are sure what you are looking at even if it turns out in the end to be a familiar picture, and its aesthetic impact will have been quite destroyed by the extinction of the peripheral field even when you have been all over it again and again. Only if you look through the pinhole at a very distant building or ship on a very clear day will you achieve any satisfactory sense of beauty and that only because the pinhole can never be reduced to a size that excludes everything but what falls on the fovea. If you try to reduce it farther it fills with what are seen as shadowy obscurities.

The impact of a work of art depends, as everyone knows, not only on the nature of all its parts but on their spatial distribution also. But that distribution is something which must always be incompletely seen because it necessarily lies in the peripheral field. To ask what a picture would be like if we could see all its features simultaneously is nearly as nonsensical as to ask what a tune would be like if we could hear all its notes simultaneously. We think we see more than we do in the peripheral field not only because of the speed with which we move our line of sight about, but also because memory soon begins to fill in a few of the peripheral field's deficiencies, and memory is constantly jogged by vision 'out of the corner of the eye' as the line of sight shifts.

Think of someone you know well. Can you visualise their eyes and hands simultaneously? Visual memories may well be so often ineffective because people try to do the impossible and visualise the whole of a thing at one and the same instant instead of part at a time. But even using the best technique, visual memory is less precise in most people than aural memory, perhaps simply because we can generally refresh visual memory more easily than aural. Most things do not suddenly disappear but sounds do exactly that and cannot be recaptured once they have died away. Thus a more precise record of them in memory is desirable, and the means to it have evolved.

The essential similarity between music and visual art may be summarised thus: in music each successive vivid sensation, the note to which the ear drum is actually vibrating, has aesthetic importance only by virtue of its relation to a context. That is our memory of the notes preceding it which have ceased to sound. In visual art each successive sharply defined sight – the sight of whatever feature the line of sight is fixed on – has, as the pinhole experiment showed, aesthetic importance, again, only through its relation to a context, and that is the appearance of the remainder of the object which is imperfectly seen in the peripheral field and is partly held in memory.

The essential difference between the two is not at all that one is received over a period of time and the other instantaneously, but that while in music the intervals of time between sensations and their sequence are of primary importance, in visual art the timing and sequence of successive fixations of the eye are of very slight importance if any. The actual spatial distribution of the features in visual art is, however, obviously very important and is somewhat analogous to the temporal distribution of the notes in music. The appreciation of temporal distribution depends entirely on memory and the appreciation of spatial distribution does so partly. It can never be present to the senses in its entirety.

It may be objected that, on the contrary, the sequence of fixations of the eye is important as is shown by the fact that a painter has power to lead the spectator's eye from one part of a picture to another and thus to suggest if not prescribe the sequence of impressions he receives. But Professor Buswell's classic study of the movements of the eye of people looking at pictures suggests rather strongly that the artist has in fact no such power.[18]

The importance of a context probably explains why no effective art of taste or touch or smell has ever been produced, although often enough attempted. The Japanese of the Heian period attempted an art of blending scents, as may be read in the Tale of Genji, while the attempt to elevate gastronomy to an art continues to be made. In both cases a succession of sensations can be prescribed but memory cannot provide an effective context for them. The taste of claret does not ring in one's head like the air of a piece of music, and when one attempts to recall it everything is thrown out of gear because one's mouth starts to water, through unsatisfied appetite. With scents there is a similar trouble in that the sense of smell cloys too easily. In both the context is far too much a mere ghost of past delights.

It is extraordinarily difficult to believe that one has never seen a work of art in its entirety, just as it is extraordinarily difficult to believe that one has never heard a tune; for we find it all but impossible to distinguish between what is present to our senses and what is present only in our mind. The mental presence feels as immediate as the sensuous one which, if we are looking, accompanies it; or if we are listening, continues it.

I do not know that many conclusions about the practice of design can be drawn from these facts, but I think that they account for certain things to be observed about the size of works of art. For example painters have often maintained that there is a 'right-size' for any particular picture, and that the painter cannot expand or contract that size without detriment to the picture. Again, a much enlarged photograph of a very minutely executed work usually makes what is evidently a travesty of it. And again, the smaller a work

18. G. T. Buswell: *How People Look at Pictures*. University of Chicago Press, 1935.

is the more important does the setting become in which it is displayed. If it is put down at random on top of a lot of insignificant odds and ends it loses much of its presence. And yet again, large works of art have usually been reckoned more 'important' than small ones. This idea is partly to be accounted for by our prevailing obsession with quantity as opposed to quality, but it has a more respectable basis than that only.

All these things are connected with the phenomena of the peripheral field. Thus the aesthetic quality of a small object and that of a much enlarged version of it are so different because most of the small object is usually seen within the central field and what parts of it lie in the peripheral field are none the less near its centre and fairly sharply defined. In the enlarged view however both what is covered by the *fovea* and the quality of the context in the peripheral field are quite different. We can see, too, that the great strength of the arts of painting, civil engineering, architecture, naval architecture and aerial architecture, as against all the arts of design on a small scale is that these arts virtually define the peripheral field. Painting does this by its boundary, architecture by its size, naval architecture and the architecture of aircraft by their isolation at sea or in the air. But in design on the small scale the peripheral field is too often confused or polluted.

As regards the equating of sheer size with 'Importance', it must however be remembered that great size is universally impressive because of its meaning. We all stand in awe of great size. The psalm 'I will lift up mine eyes unto the hills. . .' comes home to anyone who has seen a mountain. If the thing of great size is beautiful this childlike sense of awe makes the beauty more overwhelming. That is why scale in architecture is so important. If a good building is big but looks small much of its potential impact will have been lost. And as regards the destruction of a small work by photographic enlargement it must be remembered that the enlargement will often actually introduce features which the artist never intended to be seen; for it will enable the eye to resolve, that is to say separately distinguish, minutiae of tool marks or brush strokes which in the smaller original were, and were intended to be, beyond the eye's power of resolution.

The facts discussed in this chapter show that inevitably the cause of the experience of beauty is a series of events, not a state of affairs existing continuously. That perhaps is why the cause of the experience is something we find it impossible to point out. It will not stand still to be pointed at. We can point out only what we perceive. We can never point out or describe what we see.

Our piecemeal sight presents us with a succession of modifications of the appearance of whatever we look at – the series of events – and it is those which cause in us the experience of beauty. Whether the thing as it actually is would still excite the same experience if we could see every part of it sharply and simultaneously, that we cannot tell and shall never know, for that kind of seeing is forever impossible to us. Our eyes simply do not permit it. All we know of beauty comes from the thing modified, the thing incompletely seen. It does not come from the thing in its completeness.